<u>REAL</u> JUSTICE®

TED WACHTEL

The Piper's Press
Pipersville, Pennsylvania

10 9 8
First Edition

The Piper's Press
P.O. Box 400
Pipersville, PA 18947
U.S.A.

Wachtel, Ted
Real Justice
LCCN 96-092917
ISBN-13 978-096338873-5
ISBN-10 096338873-8

In memory of Ali Thurman Bonner
who served his time by turning
his life to the service of others

Contents

1

Uncle Marty's Sneaker Barn Burglary

Summer, 1978

Marty Stern, looking angry and frustrated as the juvenile court hearing proceeded, sat on the opposite side of the courtroom from me. His wife, Sharon, seemed to share his feelings but she was preoccupied with their baby daughter. I had first noticed them when they arrived that morning. I watched them throughout the day as they waited uncomfortably in the crowded hallway outside the courtroom. Marty looked at his watch again and again. Apparently no one had told him that the "nine o'clock" time cited in the hearing notification letter was the time when the juvenile court judge started hearing cases, not when the court would deal with his case. The hearing for the burglary of his retail store, "Uncle Marty's Sneaker Barn," would not occur until late afternoon.

I was as poorly informed as Marty. This was my first juvenile court hearing. As a former public school teacher I had no experience with juvenile court procedures. I was attending as a representative of the Community Service Foundation, the small school and counseling agency for troubled youth that my wife and I had established just a few months before the hearing. Two of our students, a teen-age boy and girl, along with several other teen-agers, were charged with burglarizing Marty's store.

Marty Stern also had been a public school teacher at a local high school, as well as a track coach, before opening his own retail store. As most citizens would, he expected the court to provide him with an opportunity for justice. The young burglars had waited all day in the same hallway, not far from Marty and his family. It seemed strange to me that the teen-agers were not accompanied by their parents. In the morning they seemed scared, talking nervously and smoking lots of cigarettes. Ironically, the wait outside the courtroom brought them together to plan their defense, something they never would have accomplished through their own initiative. Now they had more than six hours to contrive excuses and attempt to minimize their involvement. As the day wore on they seemed to get increasingly cocky, convincing themselves that they were going to talk their way out of their troubles.

Then, at three o'clock in the afternoon, the hearing was convened in the small courtroom used for juvenile cases. Although they were the victims, Marty and Sharon Stern had no role in the process. A police officer provided the factual information so Marty and Sharon, the proprietors of Uncle Marty's Sneaker Barn, had no occasion to speak.

The public defender did most of the talking for the offenders. When the youths did speak, their obvious attempts to minimize or abdicate responsibility were ignored by the judge, because he did not believe them. The judge put all the offenders on probation, extending the probation period for one boy who was already on probation, and remanded our two students back to our school where they had been attending voluntarily since first being charged with the offense.

After spending a day in the courthouse hallway anticipating what they hoped would be a meaningful process, Marty and Sharon experienced a court proceeding in which they had no role and which ended with ambiguous results and unanswered questions. They wondered: "What does it mean to be on juvenile probation? What does it mean for two offenders to be sent back to a school for troubled students that they were already attending? What about restitution? What about Marty's trophies and medals that were stolen? What about our feelings? Why did we spend the day waiting in the courthouse? Why weren't we asked to say anything? What just happened?" After the Uncle Marty's Sneaker Barn burglary hearing, I left the courtroom feeling terrible. I couldn't stop thinking about how isolated and confused Marty and Sharon seemed. I could only imagine how badly they must have felt. Late that night I found myself tossing and turning in my bed, still so disturbed by my experience in court that I could not sleep.

Finally, in the middle of the night, I decided to write to them. I felt I was taking a risk, that perhaps my letter would be misunderstood or unappreciated. Or perhaps they would see me as just another person in the juvenile justice system that had failed to meet their expectations.

I wrote to them about my own disappointment and dismay at how the court process failed to meet my expectations of justice. I told them how badly I felt watching them endure a day of waiting and then a hearing that seemed so incomplete and unsatisfying. I offered my condolences so that they knew that someone else recognized their plight as crime victims in an insensitive justice system.

A couple of days later, Marty responded with a phone call and we got together to talk. Although I had little but my empathy to offer, he seemed to appreciate that I noticed and acknowledged his feelings and his frustration. Marty explained that he went to court that day not seeking revenge or severe punishment for the youths. What he had hoped to get in court was a chance to talk to the kids and let them know how he felt. He particularly wanted to ask them to return one gold medal they had stolen. That medal and other trophies of his college track career had been on display in his store to confirm his credibility as a track star and coach. All the stolen merchandise and all the trophies were of less consequence to him than that one gold medal, a memento of his first triumph in college track.

But the court neither provided him with an opportunity to talk directly to the youths nor with a feeling of justice.

After my meeting with Marty, whenever I shopped at Uncle Marty's Sneaker Barn with my family, he always greeted us warmly and insisted on giving us a generous discount on sneakers. He also gave us Uncle Marty's Sneaker Barn T-shirts as gifts, which for many years served to remind me of that awful day in court.

As for the two young burglars who attended our school, their experience in court produced nothing positive. They failed to demonstrate respect for the court or the victim. Both the boy and the girl avoided their feelings by making light of the experience. For some time after the court hearing I would hear them ridiculing the judge and "Uncle Marty."

One afternoon I gave the boy a ride home from school and made an impassioned appeal for the gold medal that he and his friends had stolen. I tried to get him to empathize with Marty's feelings and I sensed that he did feel badly. But he seemed afraid to say anything.

In the years to come I would become more experienced in addressing the inappropriate attitudes and behaviors I encountered in the two students. At that time I was only a novice counselor and handled the whole situation with them in a clumsy and unproductive manner.

Marty Stern later returned to a successful career coaching college track at Villanova University. I remember my delight at seeing him interviewed on television when he was coaching American athletes participating in the Olympics.

2

Stealing the Crime

Summer, 1997

Many years have passed and our Community Service Foundation has grown to five schools, eight group homes and other programs aimed at changing the negative behavior of young people who are in trouble. But I have never forgotten the Uncle Marty's Sneaker Barn burglary and that feeling of my heart sinking at the court hearing when I first realized that our criminal justice system does not provide real justice.

If the Uncle Marty's Sneaker Barn burglary hearing had been held today rather than in 1978, the court's victim-witness coordinator would have answered many of the Stern family's questions, a clear improvement over their experience that day. In some juvenile courts today they might be asked to submit a victim-impact statement which would allow them some limited input into the decision-making process, but in other locales the judge might not ask for their input and might not even allow them into the courtroom. The criminal justice system neither serves the needs of crime victims nor provides them with a significant role in the process.

When victims do attend court, they may provide testimony, but are not permitted to talk directly to offenders. They can only listen to what offenders say when asked direct questions by attorneys or the judge. But defense lawyers curtail what defendants say and do much of the talking for them. Victims are usually unable to resolve their own emotional concerns or get the answer to the question many of them long to ask the offenders: "Why me? Why did you do this to me?"

In effect, the court steals the crime from the victim. The process focuses on determining the guilt of the offender or meting out punishment. Although the victim suffered the crime, the court defines the offense as a crime against the state and gives the judge and jury the right to be lenient or strict, to dismiss consequences for the offender or order serious punishment. Victims neither determine nor have a significant say in the outcome.

Our criminal justice system places greater emphasis on the needs of the offenders than on those of the victims because many of its practices developed out of concern for protecting the accused individual from the abuse of power by the state. English law and our own American tradition contain numerous safeguards for the rights of defendants in criminal cases. Evidence can be ruled inadmissible if obtained improperly. Offenders cannot be forced to testify against themselves. There is no equivalent tradition of concern for the protection of victims, so they are largely neglected in the criminal court process.

Furthermore, courts deal with crimes as matters of fact and evidence, with little or no regard for the emotional consequences of the crime. That is why legal proceedings usually leave victims unsatisfied and unresolved. Their needs are primarily emotional, but they have no forum in which to resolve those needs and attain closure.

When the judge transferred the Oklahoma City federal building bombing trials to Denver, he refused to allow closed-circuit television in Oklahoma so that victims and surviving family members could observe the trial. When Congress and the president made a law requiring a closed-circuit broadcast, the judge allowed only a 330-seat facility in Oklahoma City for the nearly 2,500 injured victims and surviving relatives. The victims each had to call a phone number to make a reservation for seating for one day at a time. The severely restricted seating was rotated among the large number of victims and survivors. Only a fraction of the group was able to observe the trial on any given day. The judge also assigned a retired judge to preside over the auditorium, hundreds of miles from the trial, to assure that spectators were quiet and that there was no crying.

At the O.J. Simpson murder trial the victim's sister, Kimberly Goldman, reported that had she left the trial to avoid crying during very emotional testimony she would have lost her seat. Had she brought tissues to the court they would have been confiscated as contraband.

While a crime impacts the primary victim most severely, the offense creates an emotional ripple that affects the victim's family and friends, the victim's neighbors and the community-at-large because the incident undermines feelings of safety and well-being. Courts disregard this widespread emotional impact and focus on the narrow concerns of evidence and due process. Through their lack of sensitivity to the needs of victims, their families and others impacted by the crime, courts frequently revictimize the victims and increase the psychological and emotional damage.

Victims cannot even count on seeing the offenders punished in the current system. Public prosecutors often dismiss cases because they feel they cannot win them, or bargain with defense attorneys, settling for probation or a short prison sentence in exchange for a guilty plea. Victims are often the last to know the outcome.

A woman who was part of a panel of five parents and spouses of murder victims related how, in reading the morning paper, she learned that her husband's murderer had received a plea-bargained five-year sentence (of which he served only two years). She had been told earlier by the prosecuting attorney that he had a strong case. No one from the court even had the courtesy to give her a telephone call. Criminal justice professionals are not evil but at times they are thoughtless. They have been trained and have worked in a system that was not designed to serve victims.

Nor are victims' physical losses or damages dealt with effectively. Even with the creation of state victim-compensation programs to reimburse victims, restitution can be haphazard, unreliable and unnecessarily marked by bureaucratic hassle.

Courts are all about determining guilt and handing out punishment. They are not about healing or repairing the harm. So something else, besides the court process, needs to happen to achieve real justice for victims, their families and the community.

3

Cop from
Wagga Wagga

Summer, 1994

By the time the cop from Wagga Wagga finished telling about the "Outback Vandals" and the
"Roadhouse Thief," I knew that I would be going to
Australia. I was encouraged by the hopefulness of
his stories of restorative conferencing in contrast
to my own experiences with the justice system,
which included the Uncle Marty's Sneaker Barn
burglary hearing.

Terry O'Connell, an Australian police sergeant,
was speaking at a luncheon in Doylestown,
Pennsylvania, sponsored by the Bucks County
Juvenile Court and a local alternative school,
in July 1994. He was visiting the United States,

Canada, the United Kingdom and South Africa on a Winston Churchill Fellowship, which he had been awarded for his development of a new response to juvenile crime and school misconduct called the "family group conference" (sometimes called a "community accountability conference" or "diversionary conference," and which we now refer to as a "restorative conference").

The family group conference originated in New Zealand as part of the Children, Youth and Families Act of 1989. That legislation borrowed from the Maori, the indigenous people of New Zealand, the idea of bringing together the extended family of a young offender to decide how to deal with that young person's inappropriate behavior. The new law reflected the Maori tradition that the individual's family and community should be directly involved in any response to wrongdoing, a practice typical of most aboriginal or indigenous people's response to crime.

Terry O'Connell, living across the Tasman Sea in Australia, borrowed the concept and kept the name "family group conference," but changed the procedure substantially when he adapted it to community policing in Wagga Wagga, New South Wales. Having a police officer facilitate the conference, rather than a social worker, was distinctly different from the New Zealand approach. Terry also created a written script for the facilitator to follow, which he carefully revised as he gained experience with conferencing. The script made it much easier to conduct conferences and helped ensure a reliable result. The Wagga model of conferencing also gave the victim and victim's family and friends a much greater role than the New Zealand process.

What O'Connell devised in 1991 was a carefully orchestrated emotional encounter among young offenders, their victims and their respective friends and families that typically results in a written plan to repair the harm caused by the offense. When victims and other conference participants began singing the praises of conferencing, the practice spread. The Australian media started reporting about conferences. Australian educators began using the process with incidents of school misconduct in 1994. Young offenders, if they agreed to participate, were diverted from the normal court or school disciplinary procedures.

Below are two stories Terry O'Connell told at his presentation. I found myself listening, with tears in my eyes, as he described a better way of responding to young offenders and their crimes.

Outback Vandals

A police sergeant returned to his rural community in the Australian outback to a vandalism incident that had caused a local uproar. The four offenders were young blacks who lived in the town or at the nearby Aboriginal reserve (the equivalent of a U.S. Native American reservation or Canadian First Nation reserve). They had broken into the building occupied by an all-white women's organization and trashed the interior and its contents.

Having just attended training for a new response to wrongdoing called "conferencing," the officer saw the situation as a perfect opportunity to put his new skills into practice. He also hoped that the conference would address the heightened racial tension that was a by-product of the incident.

He first contacted the offenders and invited them, along with their families and friends, to meet with the vandalism victims "to find out what happened, see how people had been affected and decide how to repair the harm." He borrowed phrases he had just heard at the training to explain the process to the potential participants. When the offenders and their families accepted his offer of the conference, he then invited all of the women victims and their respective families and friends to participate. The day of the conference was warm and sunny, typical of days in the Australian outback. This was fortunate because there were so many people in the offenders' and victims' groups that the conference had to be held outdoors. The chairs were arranged in a large circle, with the victims' group to the police officer's left and the offenders' group to the right.

The officer began by reminding all the participants that the conference was voluntary and that they could leave the conference at any time. If the victims and offenders could reach an agreement, the matter could be settled then and there. The officer went around the group and introduced everyone. Then he asked each participant a series of questions.

First the offenders were asked to tell what happened. The youths were very forthcoming in admitting what they did and in expressing regret, which immediately reduced some of the bad feelings among the victims. When the boys were asked by the facilitating police officer, "What were you thinking about at the time?" they frankly admitted their resentment of the whites in their community, a prevalent feeling among blacks, but one which was rarely expressed aloud in the presence of the whites. When the officer asked "Who do you think has been affected?" they had only a very limited view of who and how others were affected by their wrongdoing, as is usually the case with young offenders.

Then the women whose building had been vandalized told how the vandalism had affected them. They told the boys that they understood their resentment of whites, but they also admitted how uncomfortable and sometimes frightened they felt to be a small group of white people in a largely black community. Just like the black youths' resentment, the white women's feelings of fear and discomfort had rarely been expressed aloud in the presence of blacks.

Some of the victims also expressed anger, wondering if maybe the boys thought that white people could afford to repair the damage and that it would be no big deal. The most important issue, they explained, was not money; rather, the vandalism increased their fears and made them feel unsafe.

As the police officer worked his way around the group, husbands, children and friends expressed similar feelings of fear and anger. As the boys and their families listened respectfully, the intensity of the victims' group's feelings gradually subsided.

The boys' families responded very sympathetically to the victims. They apologized and expressed shame for what their children had done and promised it would not happen again. They also seemed genuinely surprised to hear about the fears and discomfort of the white minority in the community, having always felt that the whites had the upper hand. They understood how the vandalism had intensified those fears and wanted to help make things right.

By the time the conference turned to the issue of how to repair the harm, blacks and whites easily agreed to work together in the upcoming weekend to repair the damage to the building.

Both groups had gained insight into each others' feelings. The young people now realized that they had not only damaged the property of a few people, but also had affected a great many other people very deeply, including their own families.

The two groups, feeling separate from one another at the outset of the conference, now merged into one community. In the informal period after the conference, when refreshments were served, clusters of blacks and whites engaged in animated conversation. The vandalism incident had provided an opportunity for healing among people who had lived together for all of their lives without expressing their true feelings. In the safety of the conference, they had talked in a real way about how they felt toward one another and had taken significant steps toward mutual understanding.

Some of the influential blacks who lived on the reserve told the policeman how reluctant they were to call the police when there was a problem. They feared offenders would simply be locked away. They suggested that other crimes might be handled through a conference as a better response to problems on the reserve.

But I have saved the most ironic aspect of this story for last—the fact that the four vandals were only 5, 6, 7 and 8 years old. Under Australian law, the police officer had no real jurisdiction with children under 10 years old, since they were not considered responsible for their own actions. Having just learned how to facilitate a conference, however, he recognized that the process would allow him to deal with the bad feelings the incident had created in the community, even though he could not formally charge the offenders with a crime.

Had there been a number 1 in front of the boys' ages, had they been 15, 16, 17 and 18 years old, in the normal course of the criminal justice system all four would have been charged with crimes. All of them would have gone to juvenile court and none of them would have gained the kind of insight and empathy that they acquired through the conference. Blacks and whites in the community would have been left with their anger, fears and mutual resentments.

Roadhouse Thief

For months Walter, the owner of a roadhouse (an Australian term for a roadside convenience store) had noticed small amounts of money and items like cigarettes disappearing from his store. To some extent he had been in denial, finding it hard to believe that one of his employees might be a thief. Finally he secretly concealed a video camera in the store to catch the culprit on video.

Much to his surprise and chagrin he successfully videotaped Lou, a youth who worked for him, stealing a $20 bill from the drawer. Walter confronted Lou who tearfully admitted to all of the thefts during the past months. Lou was the last person Walter would ever imagine stealing from him. He was the son of a couple who were among his family's dearest friends. Nonetheless, Walter felt compelled to fire Lou from the job and call the police.

The arresting officer realized that calling the police had been a painful decision for Walter. The close relationship between Walter's and Lou's families and the youth's lack of a previous criminal record made the situation especially appropriate for a conference. Both parties agreed and the policeman convened the conference a few days later in a room at the local police station.

Lou could not have been more ashamed. He knew that he had not only betrayed people who had always been kind and generous to him, but also humiliated his own family and damaged the close relationship between Walter's family and his own.

The conference was an intensely emotional event. Walter and his wife repeatedly stated they would never have expected Lou to be the thief and how betrayed and hurt they felt. They also pointed out the distance and discomfort between their two families since discovering who had been stealing from their store.

Lou's parents echoed their friends' sentiments. They were utterly amazed that their son was capable of such wrongdoing and emphasized how ashamed and uncomfortable they felt talking to their longtime friends. They simply did not know what to say or how to make up for such a betrayal of friendship. Lou's siblings even felt ashamed at school and in town now that everyone knew their brother was a thief.

Expressing these feelings was helpful for both families and began the healing process between them. They next turned to discussing how to repair the harm and developed a written plan that satisfied all parties. As the conference reached its close, feelings eased and all acknowledged that while they disapproved of what Lou did, they still cared about him and hoped that he would eventually restore trust within his own family and with the owner's family.

Because most crimes involve victims and offenders who live near each other and are likely to continue to see each other, punishing the offender is not enough. People need personal resolution so that they can deal with each other in the future. To prosecute the young roadhouse thief through the criminal justice system would have left two families who had long been friends in a very awkward situation, unable to resume their relationship. The conference provided a way to deal with those feelings, reconcile and move beyond the crisis while squarely addressing Lou's crime.

Epiphany

During Terry O'Connell's presentation I was seized by an "epiphany," a sudden intuitive realization that I had just encountered an essential universal truth. Conferencing was so simple that it was elegant, so basic that it was complete. Nothing in my experience with young offenders could match the positive outcomes being described by this Australian police officer. I wanted to bring conferencing to North America where we lead the world in escalating juvenile crime and school misconduct. We have adopted the name "restorative conferencing" (after "restorative justice," which is discussed in Chapter 5) to differentiate the process from the original New Zealand family group conferencing model. We will use this term throughout the rest of this book.

The results with restorative conferencing were impressive. According to the Charles Sturt University study of the police experiment in Wagga Wagga, New South Wales, the number of juveniles who reoffended was half that of young offenders who were sent through the courts for the same offenses. More than 90 percent of the offenders who agreed to make cash restitution actually did so. Most significantly, victims of crimes reported almost universal satisfaction with the outcomes of these restorative conferences.

O'Connell reassured the audience of judges, probation officers and police at the luncheon that the rights of both victims and offenders are scrupulously respected in his approach to conferencing. Accused youth must voluntarily agree to a conference, but only if they admit to the crime. A conference does not determine guilt or innocence. Offenders and victims may later change their decision and opt for a court trial, even during the conference itself, although that almost never happens.

The restorative conference provides a forum for everyone in the room to speak. Young offenders hear from those they have affected, unlike in the courtroom where they routinely fail to recognize the implications and consequences of their behavior. I have often asked young offenders who are returning to our school after a court hearing, "So how was court?"

"I dunno," they usually mutter. "It was OK."

They are largely unaffected by their court experience. The judge might give them a lecture, but they almost never hear from the people most affected by their behavior—the victims, the family and friends of victims, and their own family and friends. So they leave the courtroom without connecting anyone's feelings to their wrongdoing.

In the conference, however, they are directly confronted with other people's feelings. In the early stage of the conference they are asked, "Who do you think has been affected by your actions?" and their responses are remarkably limited. They don't seem to have a clue. But as the conference proceeds their awareness grows as they hear victims, victim supporters and then their own family members and friends share their feelings and their reactions. Each conference participant has an opportunity to speak.

Emotion gives the conference its power. The feelings of family members or friends have impact. For example, the offender's young sibling might say how much he loves the offender but hates what she has done. Tears surge to the eyes of everyone in the room and the child's words touch the heart of the offender. Learning how their behavior affects others builds empathy in young offenders.

In the last phase of the conference, victims are asked what outcome they would like from the conference and the offenders are asked to respond to what the victims have requested. Victims may want only an apology or ask for financial restitution or think the offender should do community service work. Offenders, victims and anyone else in the conference may join in the discussion to help forge an agreement acceptable to both offenders and victims. The possible outcomes are as varied as the people who attend the conference.

Often the families of the offenders urge the harshest consequences to demonstrate to the victims and their supporters the shame they feel about their loved ones' wrongdoing. Victims are often remarkably generous. Having had an opportunity to vent their anger and have a say in the outcome, victims frequently feel sorry for those offenders who demonstrate genuine shame and remorse.

When an agreement has been reached, put into writing and signed by all parties, offenders may now alleviate their shame. By apologizing and making amends, by paying restitution and carrying out the other provisions of the plan, offenders can help repair the harm they have caused and be reintegrated back into the community.

After the conference, the facilitator invites all of the participants to have refreshments while the contract is being signed, copied and distributed. During this informal "breaking of bread" the participants begin the process of reintegration so that both offenders and victims can eventually shed their "offender" and "victim" identities and go on with their lives.

When I first heard Terry O'Connell, restorative conferences were being used largely as a diversion from the criminal justice system, not with serious crimes of violence. Few of us then realized how the uses for conferencing would grow. Conferences would eventually be convened after the courts had already dealt with more serious offenses as an opportunity for victims and their families to deal with their feelings and achieve healing. We could not predict that conferencing would be employed beyond schools and the juvenile justice system to respond to adult offenses or offenses in the workplace. We did not envision conferences in churches and camps and youth agencies and with parole violations and in prisons, in short, wherever wrongdoing needed to be addressed. Back then we were just learning the basics.

As I listened to O'Connell, I appreciated his explanation of conferencing because it helped me understand how the process worked. I had difficulty understanding his strong Australian accent and missed some of what he said, but found Terry to be humorous and charismatic. I certainly understood him on an emotional level and was ready to make conferencing happen where I worked and lived.

4

Australia

I felt I had found what I had been seeking since the Uncle Marty Sneaker Barn burglary hearing— a response to crime that meets the needs of victims and others who have been most affected by the offense. I imagined that we could use restorative conferences in our own organization's schools and group homes. I wanted to encourage public schools and police to use conferences with school misconduct and juvenile offenses. I didn't know how I was going to get in touch with Terry O'Connell, who would be traveling for months on his Winston Churchill Fellowship. I had encountered an exciting possibility, but I needed to know more.

My wife, Susan, who helped me initiate the Community Service Foundation, was long accustomed to my outbursts of enthusiasm, so she was not too surprised when I came home that afternoon proclaiming that I had to go to Australia. She listened intently while I explained the restorative conference process and told her a couple of conference stories. She, too, liked the concept and recognized its merit.

A few days later *The Philadelphia Inquirer* covered Terry O'Connell making a similar presentation to the Philadelphia police. The article's appearance on the front page of the Sunday edition of a major urban newspaper confirmed my strong feelings about the potential of conferencing.

Despite the media attention, Susan and I realized what an arduous task it would be to make conferencing happen beyond the boundaries of our own organization. People would have to change their way of responding to wrongdoing and adopt a whole new perception of justice.

For a few days I thought about my desire to bring conferencing to North America and the implications of that decision. That year I had finally normalized my life, after more than a decade and a half of working evenings and weekends to build the Community Service Foundation. I had recently hired a full-time administrator and was just getting used to the luxury of "free time."

Susan and I had planned a short vacation traveling through northern Pennsylvania. Before we left home, I mailed a letter to Donald Nathanson, the Philadelphia psychiatrist and author who served as the introductory speaker for Terry O'Connell at the luncheon and whose writings helped explain why conferencing worked so well. In my letter I introduced myself to Nathanson, explained that I was thinking about how conferencing might be developed in North America, and asked how I might get in touch with O'Connell or his colleagues in Australia.

Our trip through Pennsylvania afforded us time to ponder the road ahead. Susan and I understood that bringing conferencing to North America was more than a day job. If I made the commitment, while Susan continued to supervise our schools, I would have to throw myself passionately into this new effort, working many evenings and weekends again, until the project achieved maturity and viability.

Shortly after we returned from our vacation I received a phone call from Nathanson inviting us to meet with him. He had contacted the Australians by e-mail. They were interested in what I had to say.

Susan and I went to Nathanson's home. He had done some checking on us and our Community Service Foundation, saving us the task of establishing our credibility. He was already aware of our agency's good reputation and my earlier role as one of the cofounders and coauthors of TOUGHLOVE®, a national program that helps parents cope with acting-out teen-agers and young adults.

I described my vision of a nonprofit educational program that would develop high-quality trainings and educational materials to foster restorative conferencing throughout North America. Nathanson responded favorably and offered to recommend us to his Australian friends.

Nathanson gave me the e-mail address of a young academician named David Moore who, while at Charles Sturt University in Wagga Wagga, had collaborated with Terry O'Connell. Moore made the original contact with Nathanson because he felt that Don's book *Shame and Pride* helped explain the dynamics of conferencing.

David was invaluable in filling the gaps in my understanding of conferencing. We struck up a vigorous e-mail correspondence. He also sent me copies of several excellent articles about conferencing that he had written for academic publications. By the end of August I was thoroughly convinced that conferencing was all that I had hoped. I began making arrangements for my visit to Australia. My plans became increasingly elaborate and expensive. Initially I intended to talk to Australian police officers and educators who had facilitated restorative conferences and victims, offenders and their families. I hoped that I might even get an opportunity to observe an actual conference. By the time I left for Australia in November I had secured approval from our Community Service Foundation's board of directors to hire a video crew to travel with me and gather footage for a documentary on conferencing.

Arrangements were made with Terry O'Connell and his colleagues for us to videotape interviews with school, police, court and government officials, as well as conference facilitators and victims, offenders, family and friends who had participated in restorative conferences.

What I heard from the conference facilitators and participants themselves further reassured me that conferencing was a practical and reliable approach to addressing incidents of school misconduct and juvenile crime. Here are some of their stories.

Schoolyard Bullies

One Sunday Patrick was playing wall ball in the schoolyard with a friend. He hit his ball over the wall and it landed where several boys were playing basketball. They threw his ball into an adjacent fenced area instead of returning it. When Patrick retrieved his ball, they took it from him and threw it away again. Then they started punching and kicking him. The three assailants bullied him and drove him from the schoolyard, and then repeatedly kicked and hit him as they followed him almost to his home.

According to his mother, Patrick phoned her at work and was in "an incredibly distressed state." She was, of course, angry and upset, but as a professional youth worker she had an unusual perspective, often counseling boys very much like the bullies who battered her son. Her son was afraid of his assailants. He did not even want to tell anyone. But she could not abide simply ignoring the event. When she called the school the next day and the deputy principal suggested convening a restorative conference as a way of dealing with the assault, she was receptive. The conference seemed to her to be a good way to address the bullying.

The conference took place a few days later. It included the three offenders, their parents, Patrick and his mother and older sister. The conference began, as they always do, with the facilitator, in this case the guidance officer, reminding everyone that the conference was voluntary and that participants could leave at any time. She said this conference was not only an alternative to school disciplinary action, but, with the understanding of the local police, also an alternative to prosecution in juvenile court.

Each of the offenders and Patrick individually told what happened. For the offenders' parents, the description of the attack was sobering. Their boys had not only teased and bullied a school-mate, but had abused him in a way that could have caused serious injury. Everyone at the conference had an opportunity to speak about how the incident had affected them. After the agreement had largely been concluded with some very strong consequences for the offenders, and the conference seemed to be coming to a close, Patrick, who had said very little previously, indicated that he wished to speak. He sat up taller than he had been and raised his eyes from looking at the floor. "This is not easy for me," he said, "But I feel like what you are asking these boys to do is not fair. And I would like to see it changed, and this is how I would like to see it changed." He proceeded to reduce or eliminate the harshest aspects of the agreement. The rest of the group, much surprised by his sudden assertiveness, did not argue with his views and the agreement was finalized as he had requested.

In the informal period after the conference, while the contracts were being written and signed, each of the young perpetrators went over to Patrick, apologized to him and shook his hand. His mother described the apology by each of the boys as "very legitimate." She said, "It wasn't posed and it wasn't artificial. It was very real and very strong." She further indicated that her son was "able to go back to school and feel safe."

When I interviewed her for our video production, she summarized her view of the conference process: "If these young people had been charged by the law and gone through the process of juvenile court and those sorts of processes, I don't have any doubt that it would have perpetuated the process of aggression within them. I don't have any doubt that it would have perpetuated the feelings and behavior of victimization on the part of my son."

Patrick's older sister had been skeptical before the conference. "I was quite surprised actually," she said. "It really was a good way to solve the problems between people. And the kids, as far as I know, the boys that attacked my brother, they treat him a lot nicer now. They're friends with him and talk to him and stuff. It was really good."

The Egging

The day her friends threw eggs at her house, 17-year-old Alice moved out of her parents' home and in with her boyfriend's family. The egging, in addition to her many previous difficulties with her parents, brought their relationship to the boiling point. They told her to leave.

Although Alice herself had participated in the egging of other people's houses, when she learned that Helen, a longtime girlfriend had been among those who egged her parents' home, she was enraged. Mutual friends tried to cool her down, but she refused to listen. Walking down the street with her boyfriend's little sister, Alice encountered Helen. Without waiting for explanations she punched Helen, knocking her to the ground. Helen's parents insisted on bringing charges for assault. The police sergeant handling the case decided to offer a restorative conference as a way of handling the incident and everyone agreed to participate.

Since Alice was no longer living with her parents, they did not attend the conference. Instead she was supported by her boyfriend's mother and the little sister who had been with her at the time of the assault. Helen was there with her parents. A mutual friend of Alice and Helen attended as well.

At the beginning of the conference Alice apologized to Helen for hitting her, but her grasp of the implications of what she had done was limited. Not until everyone had shared how the assault affected them did Alice really begin to see the extent to which her violence harmed other people. When the conference facilitator asked the boyfriend's little sister how the incident had affected her, tears came to her eyes and she said that she had been very frightened and had cried. For Alice, that was the most poignant moment of the conference.

When Helen's angry parents heard Alice talk about her conflict with her parents and realized

that she had been put out of her home after their
daughter had thrown eggs at the house, they also
became more understanding. Not that they felt
that Alice was justified in assaulting their daughter, but they saw more clearly how the turmoil in
her life contributed to the event.

The mutual friend told the offender how angry
and shocked she was. She pointed out that Alice
had been part of egging other people's houses
and no one hit her. She also expressed regret
that their group of friends had been torn apart
by the assault.

Once the group turned to repairing the harm,
they quickly reached an agreement that included
a formal apology. This time Alice apologized to
Helen and Helen's parents with a much deeper
understanding of how many people had been
adversely affected by her act of violence.

I interviewed the mutual friend who had attended in support of both victim and offender.
She was delighted that her friends were back
on good terms because of the conference. "I was
amazed," she said, "I thought it was really good
that a policeman would actually sit down and try
to work things out in that perspective instead of
just paperwork, filing and OK, your court date's
this day. I thought this was good, that it will work,
and it did work."

Alice described to me her reaction to her boyfriend's little sister in the conference. "I felt bad,"

she said. "I made her cry. I felt low, ashamed that I'd done it in front of her, and that she'd seen me do it. That maybe she'll go out and hit one of her friends or something. I felt like a bad example."

Victim Generosity

As I interviewed the Australian conference participants, I began to realize that the conference process dramatically transforms the victims' perspective. If they have an opportunity to express their feelings and have those feelings acknowledged by others, especially the offenders, they often put aside their own anger and hurt and are remarkably forgiving.

I was particularly struck by the generosity of Mary, a woman who had her car vandalized. Only six weeks before, her car was stolen from the same parking lot. After waiting a long time for her insurance company to pay her, her new car was now damaged by three boys who wedged a fire hose in the exhaust pipe and turned the water on full blast. They also let the air out of all four tires.

The conference was convened with the three offenders. Two of the boys were brothers and came to the conference with their parents. The third boy, Will, came with his mother. Mary came by herself, although she had been encouraged to bring supporters. Apparently her husband had to be at work.

The boys began by explaining that two of them were supposed to be in school and the older brother was supposed to be looking for a job. They were wandering around town, saw the car in the parking lot next to the fire hose and started fooling around with it. One thing led to another.

Mary was angry when the conference began, but she seemed relieved to learn that her car was selected at random because it was in the wrong place at the wrong time, not because it was hers. Initially she may have feared that the vandalism was related to the car theft six weeks before. She explained how she heard that her car had been damaged, how her husband started the car and how relieved he was that more water did not get into the engine and cause substantial damage. He was eventually able to start the car after draining the oil and replacing some parts. At one point in telling the story Mary began to cry.

The parents of the two boys and Will's mother were effusive in their apologies. Then both of the mothers also began to cry, insisting that they had not raised their children to behave like this.

In the agreement phase of the conference, everyone agreed that the boys themselves should pay the costs. At this point Mary said that she didn't care if they paid a little every week, but the parents insisted that they should pay right away, that they had enough money. The two brothers apologized and paid. Will remained conspicuously silent and seemed very reluctant to pay up. He had yet to take any responsibility or express any remorse. He seemed not to care and was annoyed that he had to be at the conference. On a couple of occasions during the conference he even asked the police officer when he could leave.

In frustration his mother began to cry again. She explained that Will's father was in jail for beating her up. She said that she had been having trouble getting him to do what he was supposed to do. But eventually Will agreed and paid his share of the money also.

The conference ended and during the informal phase, the two brothers apologized again and the two mothers hugged and kissed Mary, repeatedly apologizing for what their children had done. The father also expressed his deep disappointment with his sons.

The police officer took Will and his mother aside and recommended a counseling agency that might help the two of them deal with the tough times they were going through. Will did not object.

When I interviewed Mary I asked her why she was so willing to have the boys pay a little at a time, despite the fact that she had been so inconvenienced and wronged. She said to me, "I just felt sort of guilty."

I must have shown some surprise on my face because she quickly added, "Well, not guilty. I just sort of felt sorry for them more than anything. I thought they were sorry but I didn't expect them to pay me up front. But it was the parents that actually wanted them to pay. The most important thing that came out of the conference is that they came and they were sorry for what they had done and they apologized. And they apologized quite a few times. And they gave the money, so I was happy."

Mary's generosity is more the rule than the exception. Contrary to the popular view, victims do not want revenge. If offenders show genuine remorse and agree to right the wrong, most victims are easily satisfied. More than anything, victims want to feel better.

Bearded Dragon

Sometimes conferences don't go smoothly. That usually has something to do with a flaw in preparation for the conference. Ideally the conference facilitator visits or phones every individual who will be attending. When this doesn't happen, problems may arise. In this story, which involved the killing of a wild animal on school grounds, the parents of one of the two offenders came without understanding the reason for the conference.

Bob and Allen tortured a "bearded dragon," a relatively scarce species of lizard, during the school day. Other students who observed the cruelty and ultimately the killing of the animal were very upset. After several students went to teachers and the school administration, the school decided to hold a restorative conference to deal with the incident.

The conference facilitator scrambled to invite everyone but had not been able to reach Allen's parents, nor had he prepared Allen for the conference by talking to him about what he had done. Allen had admitted to his parents that he had killed the bearded dragon, but claimed it was done as an act of mercy after his friend Bob had tortured it. So Allen's parents entered the conference harboring the feeling that their son had been unjustly accused.

Besides the two boys and their parents, the conference was attended by concerned students, some of their parents and several faculty members. The normal conference routine was upset by Allen's parents who protested the accusations against their son and the need for the conference itself. The facilitator realized his mistake in not clarifying Allen's situation beforehand, but decided to proceed anyway.

The offenders' parents heard their sons describe what they had done and then heard other students and the teachers speak, in very emotional terms, about how that kind of cruelty affected them. A few of the students cried. Some teachers spoke about the growing effort on the part of the school to help protect the wildlife in the vicinity of the school.

Both Bob's and Allen's parents were moved by the sincerity and emotionality of the students and faculty. They began to recognize that what their boys did was not just a boyish prank, but an affront to the sensibilities of many well-meaning people who wanted to protect increasingly threatened wildlife and the environment in general.

By the end of the conference the adversarial tone that began the conference had completely subsided. The two boys expressed their regret and offered to help with a tree-planting project on the school grounds as a way of demonstrating their sincerity. The anger of the other students and the faculty disappeared in light of the boys' change in attitude.

Despite faulty preparation for this conference, the process proved robust enough to allow a good outcome. Bob and Allen were forgiven by their fellow students and the incident raised the environmental consciousness of the entire school community.

No Big Deal

We often judge the emotional impact of a crime by the severity of the offense, but lesser crimes often wreak havoc in people's lives, not because of physical harm but because the crime disrupts their feelings of safety and normality.

Terry O'Connell told me a story while I was in Australia about the theft of a motor bike from the veranda of a suburban home. No big deal. Just a motor bike, not much expense, no violence. The family consisted of a mom and dad and four little girls who ranged in age from 4 to 12 years old.

Terry "rang" the mother on the telephone and asked if she wanted to participate in a restorative conference with the two teen-age boys who had been apprehended and had admitted the offense. "No, we would be too terrified," she said. "I'm going to get counselors. My family has been severely traumatized."

Terry responded sympathetically. He asked if he could come and speak to the family personally, to explain how the conference might address that fear and trauma. The mother agreed and after his visit the family eventually agreed to participate in a conference.

In the conference, the mother spoke emotionally to the boys, as did the oldest sister. Both spoke in general terms about how the theft had traumatized the younger sisters. Although they talked only in general terms in the conference, Terry later learned that the youngest sister, after the incident, started wetting her bed. Still another insisted on sleeping with her parents. The second oldest sister wouldn't go out on the back veranda after dark.

Because the motor bike was recovered, there was no financial restitution involved. The agreement focused on apologies and some community service work.

After the conference ended and the offenders left, O'Connell chatted with the family. The mother assured him that the conference had brought her family closure. She said that she had no idea how they would have effectively dealt with the aftermath of this event without the conference. The 12-year-old began to cry with her younger sisters watching her. "I felt really sorry for those two boys," she exclaimed. "They're just like the boys down the road." For she and her sisters the face-to-face meeting with the boys made the offenders real and normal, removing the fear from their nights.

When Terry followed up a week later, the mother said that the conference was a fabulous experience for the family. The girls had not stopped talking about it. The issues of trauma had not surfaced again and the family's life had returned to normal.

When I interviewed John Braithwaite, the well-known Australian criminologist, whose book *Crime, Shame and Reintegration* provides a sociological explanation for why conferencing is so effective, he told me about a conference he observed. His story further illustrates why we cannot assume that a lesser crime has only a modest impact on victims.

An elderly woman's pension check was stolen from her mailbox by a teen-age girl. At the outset of the restorative conference it became clear that the youth had assumed that the woman was in a much better financial position than she actually was and would not really miss the money.

But the girl's eyes grew wider as the woman explained that the pension check was her primary source of income. After the theft occurred she was so frightened that she spent hundreds of dollars from her modest savings to put special locks and security bolts on all of her doors and windows. And so did the other elderly woman living next to her.

The young girl was astonished by the fear and expense she had caused by her seemingly petty theft. Had this offender been prosecuted through the courts without a restorative conference, she would never have achieved this realization.

5

Restorative Justice

I said goodbye to most of my Australian friends at a barbecue in Terry O'Connell's backyard and parted company with the video crew. After nine hectic days of non-stop travel and videotaping, I had seen little of Australia except police stations, high schools and a dead kangaroo by the side of the highway, although I did meet a lot of lovely people.

As I made the long trip back to Philadelphia, I began to face the magnitude of the project I had undertaken: to implement restorative conferencing throughout North America. What had I been thinking? How audacious. How grandiose. How overwhelming.

Returning home in time for Thanksgiving gave me a chance to recover from extreme jet lag, switching from day to night and summer to winter, before resuming work. Then I began to implement what we had decided to call the Real Justice® program.

My first priority was to organize a training for the staff of our own organization, Community Service Foundation. I decided to hold two trainings, one before a weekend and one after the weekend, so that we could send half our staff one week and half the next. The Australians and I had tentatively planned a training for March 1995, which left me about four months to recruit enough paid trainees to share the costs of this expensive undertaking.

I made my first attempt at promoting Real Justice in early December, inviting a group of educators, police and probation officers to see some clips from the interviews we had video-taped in Australia. I discovered then something I would find in each one of the hundreds of presentations I would make over the next few years: There is at least one person in each group who makes the same strong intuitive connection that I did and comes away with an enthusiastic interest in finding out more about conferencing. Although I also encountered cautious skeptics, I almost never experienced strong opposition because there is something about conferencing that simply makes sense, even if one needs further convincing.

As I began my efforts, I was largely unaware of a significant factor working in my favor. Although my own instincts had independently led me to pursue conferencing, my inclination was consistent with a growing interest in North America in a concept called "restorative justice."

Although I was vaguely familiar with the term, I began to gain a deeper understanding of the concept when I went to Minnesota in January 1995 to videotape some interviews with a police department that was doing a modified version of the conferencing process developed in Wagga Wagga.

On the same trip, at the urging of Terry O'Connell, I visited with Kay Pranis, the restorative justice planner for the Minnesota Department of Corrections. I have been forever thankful for his recommendation. Kay has consistently guided and challenged me toward a deeper understanding of the significance of conferencing and its implications within the larger context of restorative justice.

Kay spent a Sunday with me, introducing me to Mark Umbreit, a leading proponent of victim-offender mediation, and showing me a videotape that acquainted me with Howard Zehr, whose book *Changing Lenses* is one of the seminal works and most helpful explanations of restorative justice available.

Zehr's background includes his Mennonite heritage of peacemaking, direct experience with offenders and their victims, and an active interest in photography, which influenced his book's title. In *Changing Lenses* he points out that we currently look at justice through a "retributive" lens, viewing crime as an offense against the state that requires punishment. He suggests that we look at justice through a "restorative" lens, recognizing that a crime is actually committed against people and the focus of justice should be on restoration of the victims' well-being.

Restorative conferencing represents the latter perspective, where we emphasize repairing the harm by addressing the emotional and material needs of victims. Conferencing includes as participants the community defined by the offense, which David Moore, the Australian academician, has defined as the "micro-community," the victim, the offender and their respective family and friends. I came to the realization that although victim-offender mediation was the dominant model of restorative justice practice at the time, conferencing more adequately matches the ideal expressed by Zehr because it includes not only the victim and offender, but also the family and friends of both. Real Justice also goes beyond the criminal justice system to deal with wrongdoing in schools, workplaces, anywhere that a more effective response would be useful—presumably everywhere.

I felt affirmed in advocating restorative conferencing and appreciated Zehr's articulate explanation of a new way of looking at justice. I especially
valued his descriptive contrast and comparison
of retributive and restorative justice, which I have
adapted slightly and expressed below as the ten
differences between Real Justice or restorative
justice and our current criminal justice systems
or school disciplinary systems.

1. In our current systems an offense is defined as
a violation against the system, as a crime against
the state. In Real Justice or restorative justice,
an offense is defined as the harm that is done to
a person or the community.
2. In our current systems the focus is on establishing blame and guilt. In Real Justice the
focus is on solving problems, on how to repair
the harm.
3. In our current systems the victim is largely
ignored. In Real Justice the victim's rights and
needs are fully recognized.
4. In our current systems the offender is passive,
but in Real Justice the offender is encouraged to
take responsibility.
5. Currently we define accountability as punishment. Real Justice defines accountability as demonstrating empathy and helping to repair harm.
6. In our current response to an offense we focus on the offender's past behavior, but in Real

Justice we focus on the harmful consequences of the offender's behavior.

7. Under our current systems the stigma of crime is largely unremovable, but in Real Justice the stigma of crime is removable through appropriate actions by the offender.

8. Currently there is little encouragement for repentance, but in Real Justice repentance is encouraged and forgiveness is possible.

9. Our current systems depend on professionals for justice. Real Justice relies instead on the direct involvement of those who have been affected.

10. Our current system is strictly rational, but Real Justice allows and encourages the free expression of emotion.

Derived from the ancient tradition of the Maori, incorporated into New Zealand law and adapted by an Australian police officer, Real Justice conferencing began in North America in late 1994 and coincided with the restorative justice movement, an ongoing effort to reform our current criminal justice system.

6

Sowing the Seeds

In March 1995, Terry O'Connell and four other Australians arrived to lead the two trainings organized by Real Justice in Pennsylvania. The twelve days they stayed with our family and next door at my sister Rebecca's home were a constant buzz of activity, both exciting and exhausting. My sons Ben and Josh, one just finished with college and the other awaiting his stint in the Peace Corps, chauffeured the Australians and others from place to place. My wife, Susan, and I attended to meals and kept things organized while our 12-year-old daughter Katie helped where she could.

Ever since I heard Terry O'Connell speak and especially since I returned from my trip, we anticipated with growing enthusiasm the arrival of the trainers who would help us launch the Real Justice program in North America.

In the four months since I visited Australia we had assembled over 150 trainees: educators, youth counselors, police, probation officers and others from Pennsylvania, Minnesota, Vermont, Ontario and as far away as Alabama. In Minnesota Kay Pranis had recruited the largest out-of-town contingent. Canadians, having encountered Terry O'Connell and David Moore on their earlier visits to North America, comprised the next largest group.

Nishnawbe-Aski Legal Services, which serves about 50 remote First Nation (in the U.S. we say Native American) communities near Thunder Bay, Ontario, sent a half dozen representatives. Their purpose was to acquaint some of the young leaders of these Cree and Ojibwa villages with an approach to justice similar to the way First Nation people responded to wrongdoing for centuries before they were forced to abandon their practices by the Canadian government. Now in an era when First Nation people are gaining greater autonomy, restorative conferencing offers a practical model for restoring a more traditional approach to justice.

Both trainings went well. Many of the trainees, including our own staff, had been sent by their agencies and were skeptical at first, but they responded to the obvious intelligence, passion and commitment of the Australian trainers. In the end most of the trainees were enthusiastic and made commitments to try conferencing in their own settings.

Seeing My First Conference

While the Australians were here for the training, I finally got the opportunity to see my first restorative conference. My previous impressions of conferencing relied on written accounts or my interviews with conference participants in Australia. Three months before the first Real Justice training three youths had thrown "Molotov cocktails" into a family's suburban home in the middle of the night. Only smoke detectors saved the lives of the father, mother, and their 17-year-old daughter and 12-year-old son sleeping on the second floor. They were awakened just before all the oxygen was consumed by the flames on the first floor. They escaped with their lives, but the entire family was traumatized, especially Tom, the 12-year-old son.

The young offenders were apprehended and admitted their guilt but the arson victims remained in shock and disarray. They were living in temporary quarters and relying on donations of clothing, food and other support from neighbors and relatives. They were further demoralized when the offenders went through a court hearing to determine whether they should be certified as adults rather than be dealt with by the juvenile justice system. The victims had to listen as witness after witness, in an effort to keep the teenagers from being sent to adult prison, told the judge how good the offenders really were. The victims also heard the suggestion that a racial slur by their daughter against one of the offenders had provoked the incident.

The victims could not respond to the allegation in that setting. They had no opportunity to ask the offenders questions, challenge how an alleged racial slur might have justified such a violent response, or present their own story. They could only listen and see the allegations and the outcome repeated in the newspapers the next day. The three offenders were not dealt with as adults, but sent to a secure juvenile treatment facility.

A forensic psychologist suggested that a restorative conference would benefit the victims, the offenders, their friends and families, and the local community, which was still shocked and unresolved. The psychologist was aware that the pioneer of Australian conferencing, Terry O'Connell, was going to be visiting the U.S. to conduct trainings and felt that his visit offered an opportunity for an experienced conference facilitator to bring healing to all those who had been affected by the crime. Terry agreed to facilitate the conference.

Because the conference is voluntary for both offenders and victims, O'Connell went through the process of inviting victims and offenders to participate. He also met with and reassured the court victim-witness coordinator and several juvenile probation officers, who were understandably worried that the conference might cause more harm than good. They were especially concerned that the unresolved issue of the racial slur would cause the conference to overheat and boil. O'Connell assured them that it would not.

As the two groups, the offenders and their family and friends and the victims and their family and friends, arrived, O'Connell directed them to two separate rooms. After seating arrangements were explained and some questions and concerns were addressed, the 30 participants entered the conference room and took their seats. The participants sat in a circle. Observers, like myself, sat out of the circle and some distance from the group.

O'Connell explained, stating the standard preamble in the script used for all restorative conferences, that the purpose of the conference was to find out how the incident had affected everyone and how to repair the harm caused by the young offenders' actions. To his immediate left sat the 12-year-old victim, Tom, facing away from the rest of the circle with an upraised arm shielding himself from any view of the offenders.

Of the victim's family, he was the one most visibly traumatized by the experience.

The group was then guided through the process. Initially the offenders were asked individually to describe the events leading up to the incident, the incident itself, what they were thinking about at the time, and what they thought about afterward. Although some of the observers had previously wondered if it would be more empowering to allow the victims to speak first, the process seemed to work well with the young offenders admitting to their misdeeds, in their own words, right at the outset.

Next the victims spoke, expressing their outrage at what was done to them. They described how they had lost everything in the fire, were living in turmoil without a home and had their lives changed forever. The mother insisted that the offenders would have to reassure her 12-year-old son that they would never hurt him again.

After all of the victims' relatives and friends expressed their feelings, Tom, who had initially refused to speak and who would not even face the circle, now turned and spoke directly to the offenders with emotional eloquence. Pouring out his anger and fear, he told the offenders that he could barely sleep, every sound startled him, every siren unnerved him, that he could hardly concentrate, and that he lived in fear that they would hurt him again. Tom said that he found himself always grumpy, preoccupied with his fears and unable to do or accomplish anything. He said that he only came to the conference because the rest of his family was coming.

The offenders sat with their heads bowed. Although some observers later commented that they expected the offenders to cry and show more emotion, those who are more familiar with the process realize that some people are not given to emotional displays. They advise observers to watch for more universal expressions of shame such as "showing the victim the top of their heads" or bowing in shame.

After the victims and their friends and family finished speaking, Terry shifted the focus to the family and friends of the young offenders. They spoke about how sorry they felt about what happened and that they could not understand how the three boys did what they did. The offenders continued to sit with their heads bowed.

O'Connell then asked the group what could be done to repair the harm. He asked the victims what they expected from the two offenders. One of the victims' friends suggested an apology as a start, and the offenders apologized. The injured mother demanded that the three offenders assure Tom that they would never do anything like this again, which they readily did. They also said that they wished they could take back what they had done. The victim father said that all he wanted was some relief from the trauma they had endured and that he felt the conference itself was helpful.

In this final phase of the conference it became clear that the two sides had become a circle, that the two groups had become one community. For example, a teen-age friend of one of the offenders, expressing concern about the effect all the publicity had on the victimized family, suggested that he and the daughter collaborate on an article for the school newspaper talking about how life has been for the victim family since the incident. Everyone agreed.

The alleged racial slur, which several participants had mentioned, failed to emerge as an issue in the conference, as some had feared beforehand. One of the conference participants said to the offenders, "I hope that you have learned from this experience, that life isn't always fair, but that taking revenge doesn't help at all."

The father of one of the offenders reassured the victims that "we are very, very sorry."

The daughter spoke of her family's determination to overcome this setback in their lives and return to a normal life. She also initiated a series of "thank yous" from participants to the facilitator, Terry O'Connell, for having convened the conference.

Immediately after the conference, members of the victims' and offenders' groups approached each other. There was animated conversation, even joking. Knowledgeable observers noted that the conference helped alleviate post-traumatic stress caused by the crime, particularly for 12-year-old victim Tom. He now stood strong and erect, fully engaged in conversation, a smile on his face.

The arson conference allowed me to experience firsthand the power of conferencing. For anger and anxiety of such intensity to give way to smiles and relief was a remarkable transformation. The victims eventually returned to their renovated home and the offenders spent almost two years in juvenile treatment facilities and group homes. Neither victims nor offenders waltzed off into the sunset. A singular event cannot eliminate all the problems related to a crime. Yet the conference was healing for individuals and the community, with a far better result than the court process.

After experiencing the arson conference and both trainings, I was more committed than ever to fostering the spread of conferencing. The seeds had been carried from Australia and planted in the fertile soil of North America. I had high hopes that conferencing would take root and start to grow.

7

North American
Stories

After the first Real Justice trainings, North American trainees began to conduct conferences. Every week we heard from enthusiastic conference facilitators—a police officer, educator or juvenile probation officer who had successfully convened a restorative conference.

Cannonball Run
Early one morning, a few weeks after the Australians conducted the first Real Justice trainings, I received a phone call from an assistant principal who wanted to know if we had any suggestions for convening a restorative conference with 75 participants—which he planned to hold

that night. I lacked the experience to answer his questions, but early morning in Pennsylvania was late evening in Australia, so I called Marg Thorsborne, a guidance officer in Queensland who had run an unusually large conference for a group of students who had slaughtered birds in a nature reserve.

With both the assistant principal and myself on the telephone line, she suggested that the chairs be configured in curved rows facing each other. The usual circular arrangement would place everyone too far from each other and the circle itself would be far too large.

She also warned that the conference would run far longer than the usual hour or so because many people would want a chance to talk. She was pleased to hear that a police officer who had also been trained in conferencing would help manage the event, ushering people into the room and attending to other details while the assistant principal facilitated the conference itself. Because of the extended time that people would be there, she recommended having plenty of snacks and beverages available so that individuals could take short refreshment breaks while the conference proceeded.

After we ended our telephone connection to Australia the assistant principal explained that for several years a group of juniors and seniors had been staging an annual "Cannonball

Run," a high-speed auto race on public roads. The race was named after an old Burt Reynolds movie and was held on the day of the high school senior awards assembly. The assistant principal and local police had tried to prevent this year's race but several students managed to either sneak off school grounds or simply did not come to school that day. Speeding through small towns on rural roads, they avoided the police until one of the racers hit another car. The occupants of the car that was struck were not seriously injured but were quite shaken by the crash.

With several of the race participants in custody, the police learned the names of all of the participants. Recently trained in restorative conferencing, the assistant principal and juvenile officer agreed that the incident would be perfect for a conference. They decided to convene the conference in the town where the accident occurred for the convenience of the accident victims and other irate citizens who had also been affected. Seventeen students, their parents and some of their siblings brought the attendance to the projected total of around 75.

The conference lasted five hours. First each student told his part in the race. Although they expressed remorse, when they heard from the accident victims and others who had been affected by the race, they began to realize the serious

consequences of their behavior. They had terrified a large number of people.

In telling me about the conference the assistant
principal described how the parents, sitting in
rows behind their sons, became increasingly upset
and ashamed. Each boy would occasionally look
back to try to catch a glimpse of his parents' reactions as the conference proceeded. Those parents
whose sons had minimized the nature of the race,
who were only cautiously cooperative or who had
some objection to the conference location, miles
from their home community, now fully appreciated
the harm their sons had done to others and the
risks that the boys themselves had taken. When
the parents had the opportunity to speak they
apologized profusely to the victims of the Cannonball Run and strongly supported whatever
consequences the group would recommend.

Because of the length of the conference, some
participants became restless. The police officer
chatted with people as they visited the refreshment table, encouraging them to see the conference through. Almost everyone stayed for the full
five hours. In the agreement phase of the conference the suggestions were written on a large flip
chart and then edited down into an acceptable
plan. When the conference ended, most people
stayed and socialized while each conference participant signed the agreement displayed on the
flip chart.

The most important item in the agreement was a promise by the students to help prevent another Cannonball Run in the future. Seniors agreed to advise younger students against continuing the dangerous tradition and juniors agreed to do the same, especially as seniors the following year.

Another significant development came as a result of the candid discussion fostered by the conference. The Cannonball Run was perceived as a symbolic protest by many youths who resented the compulsory nature of the awards assembly in which some students received awards, while the rest of the student body were required to attend. The school decided to change its awards ceremony to an evening event for the award recipients, their families and any of their fellow students who chose to attend.

There has not been another Cannonball Run.

Two-Timer

Roger, a student at an alternative school, had been driving everyone crazy with his disruptive behavior. The school typically asks its students to actively support the counselors and teachers in maintaining decorum. After months of both students and staff confronting this youth on his inappropriate actions and encouraging him to make changes, the staff had reached their limit.

Having just attended the Real Justice training, the school staff proposed to conduct a restorative conference to deal with Roger's latest classroom disruption. They limited it to the "last incident" because the staff had learned that a conference should focus on a single event. The incident might involve several elements, like someone burglarizing three houses on a single night, but should stay within a narrow time frame. Limiting the conference to one incident keeps the process focused and manageable. Although conference participants will bring up other incidents and behaviors in the normal course of expressing their feelings and talking about what happened, the facilitator should not interrupt unless they wander too far afield. If the discussion does drift, the conference facilitator merely refocuses by gently reminding the group about the incident that brought them together and the goal of repairing the harm caused by that specific event.

In deciding who will run the conference, potential facilitators must recognize when their feelings may interfere with the process and should find another trained facilitator to convene the conference. In this case the staff invited a counselor from another school to act as the facilitator. Staff members realized they felt victimized by Roger's behavior and wanted the opportunity to express how they were affected by him.

The facilitator invited Roger's father, who had frequently been involved in telephone calls and meetings about his son, and his mother who was recovering from an automobile accident and was not previously involved. When asked to nominate other supporters, Roger named several of the students who attended school with him.

The conference was convened in the evening. Roger began by acknowledging his responsibility for the recent classroom disruption. The school teachers and counselors expressed how angry and frustrated they were with him. His mother was especially emotional. She brought everyone to the brink of tears as her emotion resonated around the room. His father also expressed feelings, but Roger was particularly touched by fellow students who said that they were afraid he was going to be discharged from the school and that they would miss him.

Roger expressed remorse and was extremely motivated in the agreement phase of the conference, coming up with all sorts of practical suggestions for how he could do things differently in the future. For example, he committed to appropriately make statements or ask questions at least three times in each of his history and English classes.

In the days and weeks following the conference, he kept his commitment. Although he occasionally lapsed into old annoying behaviors, Roger responded favorably when confronted by his fellow students or program staff members. In general, both students and staff were satisfied that he had made significant changes—until he was involved in a major behavior incident on the school bus.

Roger and a girl who attended his school yelled and cursed at the bus driver when he challenged their misbehavior on the bus. Roger also kicked something on the floor near the driver's seat, which hit the driver's leg.

Given the success of the first conference and the significant changes in behavior that resulted from it, the staff decided to try a conference for the bus incident. This is the first instance I know about in which an offender was conferenced twice. However, when Roger was asked who he wanted to nominate as supporters at the conference, he insisted that this time he didn't want any of his schoolmates present. When pressed for a reason, he admitted that he was too ashamed to have them there.

The most notable moment in the conference came when the bus driver poured out his anger and disgust at Roger and exclaimed that he was so fed up with the kind of abuse he got from kids on the bus that he was going to quit his job. Roger was stunned. He truly had no idea his behavior had such an adverse impact on the bus driver. His sincere remorse moved the bus driver, who graciously accepted the boy's heartfelt apology.

Most significantly, the conference demonstrated the community-building potential of
restorative conferences—to create relationships
where they did not exist previously. The bus driver
and his tormentor became friends, developing a
positive relationship in the aftermath of a serious
altercation.

The bus driver had no further difficulties with
Roger's behavior on the school bus.

No Pinch Hitters

A basic tenet of conference preparation is that
the facilitator, not someone else, must contact
the participants. Critical to the success of the
conference is the rapport that the participants
have with the person running it. We were advised
by the Australians against letting someone else
set up our conference for us, but it was only a
matter of time until someone put that advice to
the test.

Rachel was asked by a school counselor to
convene a conference for a student he particularly liked. He wanted the conference to take
place quickly, so instead of waiting for Rachel to
contact the participants, he made the phone calls
to the participants instead. Rachel knew that
she should have called everyone but, feeling the
time pressure from the other counselor, agreed
to facilitate the conference without talking to any
of the participants beforehand.

From the moment Rachel walked into the conference room she knew she was in trouble. She entered a room full of strangers and felt no connection with any of them. As the conference began, the girl who was the offender did not take appropriate responsibility for her behavior. If Rachel had prepared the offender for the conference, she would have reminded the offender of what she said when they talked privately. But Rachel never had such a conversation with the girl. Participants interrupted each other frequently. When Rachel tried to redirect the conference, people ignored her. The offender's grandfather rambled on aimlessly while others tried to talk. At one point in the conference the offender got up, left the room and then came back again. The conference stumbled its way to some sort of agreement and an unsatisfactory conclusion.

Rachel went home and cried. She later said that the conference felt like a nightmare, but there was no way to wake up and escape it. It just went on its own way, having slipped beyond her control.

Rachel fully acknowledged her error. She allowed the other counselor's agenda to dictate the procedure, rather than follow what she knew to be correct.

The lesson from her unpleasant experience is that successful conferences are based on the relationships established before the conference begins. The bonds built by the facilitator with each phone call and each personal visit to the victim, the offender, each of their family members and each of their friends are pieces of a jigsaw puzzle that come together at the time of the conference. Anyone at the conference who has no connection with the facilitator is like a missing piece. With too many missing pieces the puzzle becomes unrecognizable.

Expectations are established by the preparatory contacts. Each person feels respected and valued as the facilitator asks for his or her voluntary participation, patiently explains the process, answers questions and acknowledges feelings. When the participants come to the conference they return that respect by taking direction from the facilitator, by staying within the bounds that the facilitator has previously outlined.

A conference is a baseball game with no pinch hitters. If you want to facilitate the conference, you have to play the whole game, and the game starts with the conference preparation.

8

Free Expression

Until you have seen Real Justice in action you might assume that those who say conferencing "works like magic" are exaggerating. But those of us who have seen a conference transform anger and hostility into cooperation and resolution find ourselves amazed and wondering "Why does it work so well?" According to Silvan Tomkins's affect theory, conferencing works so well because it provides a setting that allows for free expression of emotion, minimizing expression of negative emotions and maximizing expression of positive emotions.

David Moore, Terry O'Connell's colleague, discovered Tomkins's affect theory as it was explained in Donald Nathanson's book *Shame and Pride*. Nathanson, you may recall, introduced O'Connell at the juvenile court luncheon where I first heard Terry speak and is a practicing psychiatrist, lecturer and founder of the Silvan S. Tomkins Institute. Although I found Nathanson very interesting, I did not have direct experience with conferencing and could not then appreciate how affect theory served to explain the phenomenon of conferencing.

Affect Theory

Tomkins identified nine basic "affects" which exist in every human being. The six negative affects are disgust, dissmell (revulsion to offensive odor), anger-rage, distress-anguish, fear-terror and shame-humiliation. Surprise-startle is a neutral affect. Lastly, the two positive affects are interest-excitement and enjoyment-joy (see Figure 1). Tomkins presented most affects as hyphenated word pairs identifying a continuum or range between the least and most intensive expressions of that affect.

These nine affects are inherent in every human being. You can see them most clearly expressed on the faces of babies. Babies everywhere in the world express affects in the same way. Affects evolved as life evolved and are fundamental to our survival. Dissmell (a term coined by Tomkins), for example, is how we react when some-

Positive Affects

Interest — Excitement
Enjoyment — Joy

Neutral Affect

Surprise — Startle

Negative Affects

Shame — Humiliation
Distress — Anguish
Disgust
Fear — Terror
Anger — Rage
Dissmell

Nathanson, 1992

Figure 1

thing smells awful and it keeps us from eating something that might kill us. Fear-terror helps us respond to danger. Anger-rage prepares us to attack. Interest-excitement guides us toward what we need to know.

Unlike babies, adults have learned how to modify facial expressions to mask true feelings. Also, reactions to affects can be changed by experiences. This is what Tomkins called "emotion." Unlike affect, emotions differ between individuals and cultures. Emotion is affect after it has been acted upon by the events of our lives. Nathanson says it nicely: affect is biology, emotion is biography. However, for my purposes in this book, I use the terms affect and emotion interchangeably.

In a restorative conference there is a natural progression from negative emotions to positive emotions fostered by free expression. When the participants first enter the room, anger, disgust, distress and fear abound. As the offenders and victims relate their experience, offenders and their families feel shame. If offenders accept responsibility and victims feel acknowledged, negative emotions can give way to interest and enjoyment. Sometimes after the conference, there is even excitement and joy.

People recognize the affects displayed on each other's faces and tend to respond in kind. Tomkins called this "affective resonance" or empathy. The result of affective resonance is that the participants in the conference make the emotional journey together, feeling each other's feelings as they travel from anger and distress and shame to interest and enjoyment. As a conference facilitator, I am always fascinated by the shift toward the positive emotions that usually occurs after the offender has shown genuine remorse and the victim has had an opportunity to express feelings. When discussion turns to repairing the harm, the atmosphere is far more positive than when the conference began.

Ground Rules

The conference provides a safe place for people to freely express their emotions. Sometimes people ask me, "Don't you have to set ground rules so that people won't abuse one another?" Their fear is that emotions will flow too freely. But if the conference facilitator has prepared everyone for the conference properly, the tone is already set for the conference through initial contacts with participants. You have talked with each person individually. You have respectfully explained the purpose of the conference: to find out how people have been affected by the incident and how to repair the harm that it caused. You have emphasized that participation is voluntary and asked for their participation. You have talked in terms of providing support for victim and offenders in a difficult encounter. So you have begun to "set ground rules" with your respectful tone and the voluntary nature of your invitation, without having to verbalize rules.

Compare this approach to how a court system sends written subpoenas or how schools contact the parents of an offending student. The contacts are formal and mandatory. The tone is intimidating. But with a conference, people sense that this is a more positive and respectful way to deal with wrongdoing than any other process they have experienced. That is why they usually agree to come. That is why they stay within the bounds that you have informally set. When the conference begins, as facilitator you reiterate that participation is voluntary and that anyone may leave at any time. A key phrase in the script is, "We are not here to decide if (the offender's name) is a good or bad person." You also repeat the purpose, "To find out how people have been affected by the incident and how to repair the harm that it caused." Although it may seem repetitive, I find that the phrases that define the conference purpose later serve as a useful cue when participants' anger boils over or when they become abusive. In the spirit of Tomkins, I allow them some opportunity to freely express themselves, but then I gently intervene and minimize the negative emotion by repeating the conference purpose. Having heard the conference purpose repeated earlier, people almost always recognize the reminder that they may express only how they have been affected and they stop their abusive verbal attack.

I am certain there are dubious readers who, as they read this, are questioning why conferences don't slip out of control and perhaps become violent. Because of the facilitator's preparatory effort that does not happen. Those who agree to participate in conferences have voluntarily selected the process, so they are willing to accept the limits of the conference.

Certain Violence

Nonetheless, some conference participants arouse our fears that the worst will happen. A high school principal told me about a conference in which everyone was sure the parents of the student offender and the parents of the student victim would come to blows. Every time the conference facilitator spoke to them they ranted and raved about the other parents, demeaning them, their child and the way they had raised that child, all in the strongest terms. Some of the school faculty began to question the wisdom of the conference and feared that it would deteriorate into a screaming match or violence.

But it did not. The conference began, as all conferences begin, with the offender telling what happened. The victim's parents first heard the acceptance of responsibility by the offender and then they began to realize that there were impor-

tant details of the offender's story that differed
from their own child's version of events, details
that suggested that their own child had some
responsibility for the incident. In fact, they found
the offender very believable. When the victim and
the victim's parents spoke, the offender's parents
also realized that they had misunderstood some
of the circumstances. When each of the parents
talked about how the incident had affected them
and admitted having made some assumptions
that were not accurate, the other parents recognized that they themselves had acted in the same
way. Feelings of anger and mistrust changed to
mutual understanding. The principal reported
that the parents were so engaged in conversation
after the conference that he had to usher them
out of the building and left them standing on the
school steps, almost oblivious to his departure.

Hostile Mothers

Although I am certainly not aware of all the
conferences that have been convened in the
United States and Canada, I am in a position
to hear about a great many. The worst of those
conferences, in terms of excessive anger, was run
by a police officer who found the mothers of the
victim and offender to be extremely hostile and
uncooperative. The mothers blamed and argued
and, unlike most conference participants, interrupted each other and yelled. Finally a senior

police officer observing the conference suggested that the conference participants take a brief recess, just to cool things down. While they were in the hall the two mothers discovered that they had gone to the same high school. The coincidence of going to the same school was helpful and the recess itself dramatically emphasized the need for more appropriate behavior. When the conference reconvened it proceeded to a positive conclusion.

Of course, not all conferences run perfectly. Occasionally the offenders do not express remorse or do so only minimally. In those cases, victims at least get the opportunity to express themselves, even though they don't get what they had hoped to get from the offenders. A good conference facilitator prepares victims for that possibility. Nonetheless, being given the opportunity to express their feelings can be very important to victims.

Getting Nothing Back

Many victims want the chance to talk directly to their offenders, even if they get nothing back. This was dramatically highlighted for me during the much-publicized trial of Olin Ferguson. Ferguson randomly shot and killed passengers traveling on a crowded Long Island Railroad commuter train. Despite the public nature of his crime, with innumerable witnesses, Ferguson proclaimed his innocence. Obviously insane, he nonetheless served as his own defense attorney at his trial. Each day of the trial I saw witnesses and survivors interviewed on television express-ing their satisfaction at having had the chance to speak directly to the offender, unlike the normal proceedings where attorneys would have sepa-rated the offender from the victims. Clearly the victims were getting nothing back from Ferguson. He was living in another reality. Yet even without Ferguson expressing remorse or acknowledging his actions, the opportunity to address the killer was helpful to many of the people who had been terrorized by his mad rampage.

The victim must have the ultimate choice of whether or not to confront the offender. Some will not choose the opportunity. Others may prefer to wait. But under our present system of justice victims and those who care about them almost never get the chance to express themselves di-rectly to the offender.

9

Shame

Some people have confused conferencing with recently publicized efforts by some criminal court judges to shame offenders into changing their ways—a modern-day equivalent of the 17th century practice of making adulterers publicly wear a scarlet letter A on their clothing. The confusion arises from the use of the word "shame" in association with conferencing. The critical distinction is between stigmatizing shame and reintegrative shame. Reintegrative shame is a concept of the Australian criminologist John Braithwaite. His book *Crime, Shame and Reintegration* was coincidentally published in 1989, the same year that New Zealand initiated family group conferencing.

Reintegration

While Tomkins's affect theory, as articulated by Donald Nathanson, serves as the psychological explanation for the effectiveness of conferencing, Braithwaite provides the sociological explanation. Braithwaite observes that those societies that reintegrate, rather than stigmatize, offenders have the lowest crime rates. Even without the extremes of a scarlet-letter approach, our current justice and school disciplinary systems deal with offenders in a way that makes it difficult for them to shed their "offender" label. We punish, fine, reprimand, incarcerate, detain, suspend and expel, but pay little or no attention to repairing the real harm done to the victim and the community. On the other hand, restorative justice strategies like conferencing allow offenders to make amends, repair the harm, apologize, gain acceptance and be reintegrated into the community.

Shame, Tomkins teaches us, is a fundamental affect and occurs spontaneously. A conference is not convened for the purpose of shaming someone; rather, shame arises automatically and naturally in offenders and their families when confronted with the reality of the offenders' wrongdoing. No matter how a society addresses wrongdoing, the act of doing so will inevitably foster shame. But Braithwaite advises that the experience should be *reintegrative, not stigmatizing*. He warns that failing to reintegrate offenders only encourages the development of negative subcultures.

We commonly see evidence of growing negative subcultures gathered on urban street corners or in schools. Youths who see themselves as "bad" align themselves with other youths who have negative self-images. Among the latter, being "bad" is a badge of honor. No longer identifying themselves with the mainstream, they reject mainstream values. Clearly something is wrong when so many feel like outcasts in their own communities. We need to reassess whether our current approach to wrongdoing is making things better or worse.

Braithwaite, as a criminologist, adopted a novel approach to the question of crime. Rather than asking "Why do criminals do the wrong thing?" he asked, "Why do most people do the right thing most of the time?" His conclusion is that most people do the right thing because they want to please the people they care about and avoid displeasing them. So the opinions of family and friends are a powerful source of social control, especially when we are young. As adults, most mature human beings have internalized this dynamic into the form of a "conscience." As adults we do the right thing because we believe in doing the right thing. But fear of being shamed, of displeasing those who love and care about us, still serves to reinforce our sense of right and wrong.

When we videotaped an interview with Braithwaite in Australia he talked about the Maori, the indigenous people of New Zealand, whose practices influenced the initial development of conferencing. "For them the Western way of transacting justice is barbaric," he said. "To have the offender stand alone, isolated, confronting the guilt of his offenses, is an act of barbarism. And their conception of shame, the Maori conception of shame, *whakama*, is the shame that you feel in the eyes of your community. It's not the Western idea of individual guilt. It's a communitarian kind of shame. And therefore, they say that what ought to happen is that the accused person ought to stand surrounded by those who love and care for him, those who are respected by him. They're the people who can shame effectively and they're the people who can offer social support during a difficult time."

I have been repeatedly advised that this approach is typical of native or aboriginal peoples around the world. An African woman at a talk I gave in Philadelphia told me that the restorative conference resembles the process her father, a chief, would conduct to address a crime in his community. I mentioned earlier that the representatives of Cree and Ojibwa villages who came to our Real Justice trainings spoke about the similarity with their traditional practices and I have heard Navajo and other Native Americans concur. Long before modern societies developed their stigmatizing practices, we allowed offenders to be reintegrated into their communities. Perhaps we need to return to what we left behind.

Tomkins said that shame is "one step removed from heaven" because shame can exist only when someone wants to re-establish a bond. Offenders must care about their relationships with others to feel shame. Our criminal justice and school disciplinary systems fail to capitalize on the opportunity to use that shame in a constructive way. They stigmatize and alienate offenders, driving them toward the other outcasts in our society who comprise the growing negative subcultures.

Compass of Shame

Donald Nathanson defined four general patterns or "scripts" to describe how people respond to their shame: *withdrawal*, *avoidance*, *attack self* and *attack other*. He organized them as the four directions on a "compass of shame" (see Figure 2). *Withdrawal* is marked by escape, by running from the shameful situation. *Avoidance* involves trying to ignore the shame, perhaps by using drugs and alcohol or distracting oneself with pleasurable indulgences. *Attack self* involves blaming or feeling disgusted with oneself. *Attack others* involves displacing the feeling of shame by blaming someone else.

The Compass of Shame

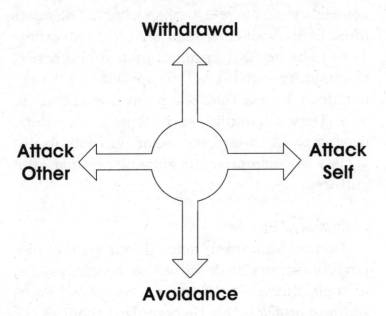

Nathanson, 1992

Figure 2

The four scripts are normal reactions to shame, but in excess they are very destructive. We can see young wrongdoers accumulating burdens of shame, usually first in school and then in the community. They demonstrate all four patterns on the compass of shame, increasing as each new offense brings greater stigmatization and alienation from mainstream society. Drinking and drugging, joyriding in cars, running away from home, missing school, lying and making excuses, blaming others, attempting suicide, bullying and committing violence are some of the harmful vehicles young offenders choose to travel in all directions on the compass of shame. Conferencing, on the other hand, addresses wrongdoing in a way that allows young offenders to resolve their shame by making amends, repairing the harm they have caused and earning acceptance and often forgiveness. If, at the earliest grade levels in schools, children's inappropriate behavior were systematically challenged with a reintegrative response, such as restorative conferencing, many would never begin their climb up the ladder of stigmatization and alienation.

10

On Our Own

We invited the Australians back to do trainings one more time in October 1995. We had 150
trainees in Pennsylvania and 200 in Minnesota,
more participants than we anticipated, but in
our enthusiasm for conferencing we felt reluctant to turn anyone away. To deal with the large
number of trainees we asked individuals who had
facilitated conferences since the first training to
help as "coaches" when small groups of trainees
role-played restorative conferences.

From the outset we recognized that we could
not afford to keep flying Australians back and forth
across the Pacific and would have to develop our
own training capability. Our first efforts began

before the Australians returned for their second visit. We converted the printed materials that had been distributed in loose-leaf format at the first training into a training manual that we had printed and bound as a book. We also produced a video that showed an actual restorative conference conducted by a police officer for two young female shoplifters. Both the manual and the video were helpful new educational resources for trainees.

As I parted ways with my Australian friends at the Minneapolis-St. Paul airport, I knew we were on our own and I felt a heavy burden of responsibility. Not only did my staff and I have to gain more experience with conferencing ourselves and then learn to train others, but we had to develop an economically viable program to sustain our mission of spreading conferencing across North America.

Training and Educational Resources

Starting with a training for a group of elementary school educators in February 1996, we began a careful and systematic effort to refine the training program originally presented by the Australians. After each successive training we scrutinized the participant evaluations, compared our own perceptions with one another and then made changes.

Our long-term goal was to develop a facilitator training that could be licensed to government or nonprofit agencies throughout Canada and the United States, so that the training effort could be localized and the cost dramatically reduced. We saw our Real Justice program as developing the training, the educational resources, the training-of-trainers and the ongoing support system.

We developed a series of "mini" role plays for the training that would allow participants to practice facilitating conferences. Each successive role play grows more difficult as the training progresses because we spike each with more difficult challenges for the conference facilitator. In the first role play the characters' roles are cooperative but thereafter some individuals become abusive or get the group off track, problems that occasionally arise in real conferences. We produced a 17-minute introductory videotape, which we sell for a nominal fee as a resource for anyone who has to present the concept of restorative conferencing. We also developed four videos for the training program. Trainers are provided with a detailed, step-by-step outline, accompanied by a set of overhead projector transparencies. The outline spells out how to set up the room, defines the goals for each training segment, and cues trainers for each of the transparencies and videos. Our goal was to make the training outline, resources and training-of-trainers so comprehensive and of such high quality that trainers consistently offer a good experience.

Research and Evaluation

At about the same time that we began to develop our own training program, we also initiated
our own research effort. The only evaluation of
conferencing for juvenile offenses to date had
been done in Wagga Wagga, New South Wales.
Another substantial evaluation was underway in
the Australian Capital Territory for both juvenile
offenses and adult drunk driving. We wanted an
evaluation of conferencing in the United States.
We were fortunate when a police lieutenant in
Bethlehem, Pennsylvania, approached us about
training officers to conference juvenile cases and
applying for research funding from the National
Institute of Justice, a division of the U.S. Department of Justice.

I had just met Paul McCold, a college professor and researcher, who was passionate about
restorative justice and enthusiastic about collaborating with me on a grant proposal. The
Bethlehem police commissioner strengthened our
research design by allowing us to randomly as-
sign cases either to conferencing or to the courts.
Much to our delight, our proposal was approved
for funding.

Bethlehem sits on the boundary of two coun-
ties, so we had to get approval and cooperation
from two juvenile probation departments, two
juvenile court judges, two district attorneys and
a number of district magistrates who handled the

offenses that are not referred to juvenile court. We reached agreement on the range of offenses that could be conferenced, including shoplifting, simple assault, disorderly conduct, vandalism and other lesser juvenile offenses.

The research project got under way just as our first trainings commenced. We were now on our own without the Australians' assistance and we seemed to be getting off to a good start.

11

Police

The first family group conferences in New Zealand were facilitated by social workers. Not until Terry O'Connell, the Australian cop, devised his own version of conferencing did police officers become involved as facilitators. There have been critics of police conferencing ever since.

When I was just starting Real Justice, a woman who was trying to initiate a victim-offender mediation program in a nearby county disparaged the idea of police facilitating conferences. "Don't police have better things to do?" she asked.

An academician warned me about "cop culture." He and others advised that police officers do not have the right temperament and mind-set to facilitate conferences. "They are attracted to policing by a need for power and authority," they said.

Others criticized the practice of police officers facilitating restorative conferences because police represent the power of the state and cannot be neutral. These critics insisted that conference facilitators, as in many victim-offender mediation programs, should be trained citizen volunteers so that neutrality can be assured. They expressed the fear that police will become both judge and jury.

Still others warned that police are not adequately sensitive to victims and their needs. In their effort to pull together the conference, police may pressure victims into a conference when they don't really want to participate.

I believe that these generalizations about police are unkind and unwarranted. While one might fairly describe the male-dominated profession of policing as more "macho" than most occupations, the police officers I know want to help people and want to make their communities safe. They are attracted to conferencing because they see its potential in helping victims get satisfaction and making offenders realize the harm they are doing in a way that the courts fail to do.

Problem-Oriented Policing

To say that police officers have "better things to do" contradicts the most progressive current thinking, such as Herman Goldstein's concept of "problem-oriented policing," which envisions police officers working as problem-solvers with the community, rather than only as law enforcers. Consider how the police officer's time is spent waiting outside courtrooms to testify in hearings that neither impact the offender nor serve the victim. Is it not better to use a police officer's time to conference a variety of offenses within days or weeks, rather than months, and achieve meaningful outcomes for victims, offenders and the community? How can anyone say that police have "better things to do"?

Those who suggest that citizen volunteers would be more neutral than police officers in running a conference confuse conferencing with mediation, where two parties of equal moral standing come together to resolve their differences and the third-party mediator avoids taking sides. Conferences involve situations where one person commits a crime or wrong against another and the two parties are not of equal moral standing. Given that the offender has admitted the offense, which is the prerequisite for holding a conference, then the victim has been wronged and the conference facilitator cannot, in all honesty, be neutral. The facilitator only needs to be fair. The person setting up the conference, whether a police officer or a civilian, must treat all the parties, including the offender, in a respectful manner. Those who

worry about the police officer becoming both
judge and jury simply do not understand conferencing. First, the offender has already admitted
his or her guilt before coming to the conference.
Second, the conference participants and not the
facilitator are responsible for deciding the outcome. Only the victim and offender need agree.
The process has no resemblance to a courtroom
proceeding.

When police have inappropriately interfered
in the conference, based on the experience of the
researchers in the Bethlehem police conferencing
project, it has happened during the agreement
phase of the conference. Sometimes police facilitators recommended that the group consider
community service for the offender when none
of the participants suggested it. Although the
facilitator is not supposed to intrude into the
discussion with such a comment, citizen volunteers and other facilitators are as likely to do the
same thing.

With respect to concerns about how police
might treat victims, one of the fundamental les-
sons taught in the Real Justice facilitator training program is respecting the wishes of victims.
There is no reason why police officers would be
any less likely to hear that message than anyone
else. The research supports that conclusion. At
no time in the Bethlehem police conferencing
project did researchers find evidence of police

facilitators pressuring victims into attending the restorative conference.

Restorative justice advocates must include police officers, who comprise the largest group of criminal justice professionals, in their vision of the future. To fail to do so risks keeping restorative justice at the margins of the system. As Herman Goldstein learned from observing Chicago police in their daily routine, police officers have a wide range of discretion in the administration of justice. Their interactions with the community provide innumerable opportunities for a restorative, rather than punitive, approach to justice.

Real Justice can transform the role of police. Police officers are extremely open to conferencing once they see it work with their own eyes. "I've been a detective for 20 years and I was a bit cynical about it when I first heard about it," admitted an Australian police supervisor in an interview with me. He continued, "I thought it was a bit too airy fairy. And we looked at it and it was fully explained to us. And I was very keen to sit in on one of the conferences to see how it went before I made the decision. Having sat in on two in one night, I was quite surprised how well they went and how the people interacted and responded to it. And from there on it was full ahead with it."

I have seen cop after cop respond to conferencing first with professional skepticism, then with

interest, finally with enthusiasm. A Bethlehem
police officer came to our very first training and
tried conferencing shortly thereafter. His enthusiasm was contagious. Soon his department's
leadership decided to implement conferencing
on a larger scale and collaborate on the research
project. He said, "Conferencing is the most powerful experience I have had in my past 20 years of
police work. It is very positive for victims in that
they are able to have a say."

Similarly two Indianapolis police officers came
with skepticism to a Pennsylvania training, but
went home determined to try their own conferences. Without formal procedures in place to
support conferencing, they had to find time to
fit the conferences into their busy day. But their
first efforts were extremely gratifying. Since then
they have become Real Justice certified trainers and are part of a major effort to implement
conferencing in the educational and criminal
justice systems in Indianapolis and surround-
ing areas.

The RCMP (Royal Canadian Mounted Police)
has taken a different approach to implementing
conferencing. In those communities where they
contract to provide local police service and in their
involvement with aboriginal policing, the police
develop a pool of community volunteers to run
the conferences for the cases that they will refer
to the volunteers.

In Sparwood, British Columbia, an RCMP sergeant and a defense attorney read an article about conferencing and decided to try it. The results have been remarkable. In most Canadian communities about 40 percent of juvenile offenders are rearrested. In Sparwood, where virtually all their juvenile cases in the last two years have been referred to conferencing and none to the courts, rearrest rates have plummeted to 8.3 percent in 1995 and to 2.9 percent in 1996.

Stolen Whale

Some police officers use conferencing more informally when it is not practical to convene a larger formal conference. My favorite example is the story of the stolen "whale." That's the way the report came over the radio—a report of a stolen whale. The police officer even checked it on his car's computer. He still read "whale." When he arrived at the indicated address and spoke with the victim, he realized that the man's southern accent had been misunderstood in the Midwestern town. Not a "whale" but an ornamental "well" had been stolen from his front yard. The officer soon apprehended Charlie, a teen-ager who admitted taking the well as a prank. While the officer wanted to handle the offense with a restorative conference, he learned that the victim was about to leave town for a couple of weeks on a vacation. So he held an impromptu conference then and there. Sitting in the victim's living room, Charlie talked about what he had done and then the officer asked the man to tell how the offense had affected him.

As is often the case with a so-called "minor" offense, the effect on the victim is far more substantial than the degree of economic loss. The real consequence is about a loss of safety, a sense that one's private space has been violated and a fear of further violations. Given that the man was about to leave town, he was particularly fearful that other theft or damage might occur in his absence. To Charlie the theft of the well had been funny, but to the victim it was deeply disturbing. The theft also came at a hectic time when the man was rushing to make arrangements for his vacation. He still had many things to do, including finding someone to cut his lawn. Charlie offered to cut his lawn for him while he was away and an agreement was quickly reached.

Charlie sincerely apologized for what he had done, now aware that his action was far more hurtful than he had ever imagined. The victim generously accepted the apology, much relieved that the incident had been resolved. Now he no longer worried about further theft or damage and he had someone to cut his lawn while he was gone.

The police officer had demonstrated a classic example of problem-oriented policing. The citizen later told all his friends and neighbors about the creative response to his problem, enhancing the community's view of the police. Charlie learned an important lesson and waved to the police officer whenever he saw him on patrol. And the police officer cruised by the house during the man's vacation and saw that the lawn was neatly mowed.

Runaway Couple

Other examples of problem-oriented policing include situations when the young person's behavior is not technically a crime, but some kind of response would be helpful. Two pairs of distressed parents reported that their respective son and daughter had run away together. The teen-age couple were found and returned to their home community a few days later. Ordinarily the police officer would have simply handed them over to their parents, explaining that there was nothing more he could do. But having learned to facilitate restorative conferences, the police officer realized that he could provide a meaningful service to the families and offered to run a conference. The parents and children agreed and the officer used the conferencing script to foster a meaningful dialogue for both families. Without attacking or accusing, but with tears flowing, each mother and father shared their feelings and fears with their children and recounted the hell they had experienced. The conference was far more effective than any punishment because the boy and girl saw the harm they had done to their parents. Rather than feeling resentment, they felt empathy.

True Confessions

It is remarkable how conferencing creates an atmosphere of genuine remorse and truthfulness, unlike the adversarial atmosphere of the courtroom where lawyers advise their clients to say as little as possible. A police officer was facilitating a conference for burglary of a retail store and suddenly, in the midst of the emotional exchanges between victims and teen-age offenders and parents, the offenders began to admit to other offenses. Lots of offenses. Not just their offenses, but those of friends. By the end of the conference dozens of burglaries had been explained, leading to a series of investigations and further conferences. Although there are legal limitations on the use of information obtained within the context of the restorative conference, the police officers in this case were able to use the information in a way that eventually resolved a great many thefts.

Police and other conference facilitators also have to be alert to revelations of abuse, which must be reported to the appropriate authorities, and to other issues that arise, like persistent conflict between parent and child that suggests the need for counseling. Police officers doing conferences may give parents and young people information about human services available in the community.

Some police have tried conferencing neighborhood disputes in which both sides have wronged one another. While police officers often intervene informally in such disputes, a properly prepared conference can provide a structured environment. Ideally the officer can get both parties ready to admit some responsibility for wrongdoing before the conference. The officer then uses the questions in the conference script to get both parties talking in terms of how they have been affected by the grievance, rather than simply accusing the other person. Parking spaces, barking dogs, noisy gatherings—these are issues that can lead to problems and violence unless people start to talk to each other in a real way and recognize each other's feelings.

Implementation

As police begin to use conferencing more systematically, different approaches to implementation are being tried. In Wagga Wagga, for example, there was a sergeants' committee that reviewed all of the juvenile cases for the week and decided which cases should be conferenced. The committee review had some indirect benefits in making officers more careful about their arrests. When the real offense was "contempt of cop," that is, when a youth was not adequately respectful of a police officer but committed no real crime, such an inappropriate arrest would be more readily detected when it passed through the hands of the sergeants' committee. According to Terry O'Connell such instances became less common.

Other police departments have assigned an individual officer to supervise cases, either by conferencing appropriate offenses himself or assigning them to other trained officers. Some departments limit conferencing to a few specialists while others have trained a large number of officers who conference cases in addition to their other responsibilities.

Police departments who do conferencing define a range of cases permissible for conferencing, usually having reached an understanding with officials of the court, such as the public prosecutor, public defender, juvenile court or president judge, or juvenile probation chief. In those communities where schools are doing conferencing, it is necessary to define which offenses may be handled within the schools themselves or by police officers who are assigned to the schools. Because conferencing is so new, most of the procedures and protocols are new and may evolve as time goes on.

Research Results

The Bethlehem police conferencing research project showed lower rearrest rates for offenders who chose conferences than for those who did not, making conferencing an excellent strategy for diverting youth from the criminal justice system. The study found that 96 percent of victims and 97 percent of offenders were satisfied with the conference process, with about half feeling "very satisfied," and 94 percent of the offenders completed the restitution and community service commitments they made in the conference. Significantly, the results of this first evaluation of conferencing in North America confirm the equally positive results of earlier research with police conferencing in Wagga Wagga, New South Wales, Australia, completed in 1995, and the preliminary results of a four-year study of police conferencing currently under way in the Australian Capital Territory with juvenile offenders and adult drunk drivers.

Also, the proportion of cases in the Bethlehem police conferencing study in which victims and offenders agreed to participate in conferences was higher than those agreeing to participate in victim-offender mediation (VOM), based on earlier studies of VOM, a restorative justice process that has been employed since the 1970s. These findings do not support the concern raised by some critics of police conferencing that victims and offenders are less trusting of police than of the trained volunteers and professionals who conduct VOM programs. The Bethlehem police conferencing study also found that conference participants reported a higher rate of satisfaction and sense of fairness than those who answered identical research questions in those earlier VOM studies. The research clearly supports the contention that conferencing by police is worthwhile. So, in answer to the critics, no, police do not have better things to do.

12

School

Schools are the breeding grounds for our society's negative subcultures. Schools do not intend to hurt children, but like much of the rest of our society they often respond to wrongdoing with punishment. They operate under the false expectation that punishment causes children to change their ways. The result of all those punitive writing assignments, detentions, suspensions and expulsions is a growing number of young people who see themselves as outcasts, as "bad." School disciplinary procedures, as in the criminal justice system, provide little or no opportunity for reintegration—for making amends, apologizing, repairing the harm or shedding the offender label. They exclude from the disciplinary process those most affected by the offense—the offenders, victims and their respective communities of care. The primary difference between schools and courts is that schools start alienating offenders at an earlier age.

Educators are no more to blame than anyone else. We all have grown up in a punitive system and have rarely questioned it. Like our politicians, school administrators keep trying to satisfy a concerned public by being tougher and punishing more severely. And we all have watched in dismay as outrageous behavior becomes more commonplace, despite police in the schools and an all-time high in the number of expulsions.

We must rethink our assumptions, not our goals. We must still demand appropriate behavior and accountability, but we can no longer rely on school administrators dictating outcomes. Rather, we should make offenders face the real consequences of their offenses by involving everyone who has been harmed. Family, fellow students and faculty members who have been affected need a forum to tell the offenders, in emotional terms, how they have been affected by that offender's inappropriate behavior.

The first restorative conference in a school setting took place in Australia at Maroochydore

High School in Queensland in 1994. Since then conferencing has been used to respond to a wide variety of problems in elementary and secondary schools.

Pepper Mace

Two boys sprayed a whole can of pepper mace on classroom door handles in a high school hallway. The odor was so pervasive that hundreds of students were evacuated from the building, with some students and faculty experiencing serious allergic reactions to the caustic fumes. The police had been contacted, so when the two youths were discovered and admitted their offense, the normal administrative response would have been to press criminal charges and suspend or possibly expel the students. Instead, a school district social worker who had been advocating for Real Justice was invited to facilitate a restorative conference with parents, faculty who had to evacuate the building and school administrators, who all felt very much victimized by the youths' actions. The formal outcome of the conference included written apologies and community service work for both youths.

The informal outcome was of greater significance, as expressed by the assistant principal whom I interviewed many weeks after the event. As the school disciplinarian, he acknowledged that he had dealt with the boys before, one in particular. He felt that the boy never fully appreciated how he affected other people with his previous misconduct. He was extremely pleased with the conference and believed, not only that the boys were genuinely remorseful, but also that they really understood the harm they had done to a great many people. He reported that all of the administrators and faculty were pleased to have had an opportunity to vent their feelings. The conference had satisfactorily resolved the matter.

Phone Prank

In another high school incident, a girl suddenly found her face stuck to a pay phone's earpiece that had been coated with a fast-drying glue as a practical joke. The perpetrators, who thought the incident was incredibly funny, gained a whole new perspective from the restorative conference. They had to face their victim and hear her describe her terror when she first realized what happened. She described how pieces of her skin remained stuck to the phone when it was finally removed. Her emotion in retelling the story resonated in them. They felt her fear and pain and embarrassment. Had they been suspended from school, their resentment would have shielded them from their victim's feelings and a real understanding of what they had done to another human being.

False Rumor

In another school several boys deliberately spread a false rumor that a girl had been masturbating during class. By the next school day the story was all over the school. When one of her friends told her, she burst into tears, then sought out the guidance counselor for advice.

With the support of the school administration, the guidance counselor decided to conference the incident. She realized that having the boys punished would distract from the real issue, the humiliation they had caused this young woman. If the focus shifted to punishment, there would be debate on whether it was too strong for what some might regard as a mere youthful prank or too light.

The guidance counselor did not contact the parents directly, which she knew was contrary to normal conferencing procedure. Rather, she called the boys into her office and told them that she had heard about the rumor and wanted them to come in with their parents to the school the next day. As she subsequently related to me, she found herself wondering about the conversation at the dinner table when the boys tried to tell their parents why they had to come to school the next day.

The conference was very powerful. No one could even think of minimizing the impact on the girl after she tearfully related how she came to hear about the rumor and how terrible she felt. She wondered why they did this to her. One of the boys' fathers had tears in his eyes and everyone in the room was deeply moved. When it came to deciding the consequence, the girl simply said, "I don't want you to do anything. I just want it to end." That was that. The boys and their parents apologized profusely and everyone left the room. They all went back to their daily activities, but not as if nothing had happened. Although no one was punished, the girl felt better because her feelings had been acknowledged by everyone at the conference. Without the boys promoting the rumor, it faded away.

Elementary School Incidents

In younger grades, conferencing is equally effective. One of the first elementary school conferences I heard about involved a serious assault by a third-grade boy against a fourth-grade boy on the playground. The conference, which was also attended by the boys' mothers, had a powerful impact on the offending boy and his subsequent behavior.

People ask how young an offender can be successfully conferenced. I suggest that as soon as children can talk and understand language, they can be meaningfully involved in a conference. I am aware of a kindergarten child being conferenced for trying to trip the secretary in the elementary school office. Although his mother was resistant to the event and after the conference referred to it as a "kangaroo court," the little boy was pleased. He told some of his classmates how glad he was that the conference helped him and that he was no longer in trouble. His mother later admitted that the conference was a good experience for her son.

The little boy in question is exactly the kind of child who begins the downward spiral into negativity even as he begins his school experience. His negative behavior is punished and early on he gets a reputation as a "bad kid." Feeling like a bad kid and having no clear path to redeem his reputation as he moves through his school years, he eventually seeks the company of the other "bad kids" in his school who reinforce each other's negative behavior.

Children need limits and effective discipline. We do not serve children well if we are permissive and fail to confront inappropriate behavior. Confronting that behavior in a reintegrative way is far better than punishing and labeling children.

Role Plays as Prevention

We do not have to wait for children to do something wrong to help them gain empathy and insight into the harm caused by violence and other misconduct. Elementary teachers and guidance counselors are beginning to use role plays of

conferences as a prevention technique. I observed
a role play organized by an elementary guidance counselor in a sixth-grade classroom. The
imaginary but commonplace incident involved a
girl who had been consistently ridiculed by two
boys in her class to the extent that her parents
called the school when she said she didn't want
to go to school anymore. Beforehand the guidance counselor had discussed the concept of role
play with the students, described the role-play
incident, asked for volunteers to assume roles,
and then gave those who had roles some time to
discuss how they thought the individuals would
feel and what they might say.

The next day the role-play conference was
convened. The conference participants formed a
circle in the center of the room with the guidance
counselor acting as facilitator. The rest of the
sixth-grade class and invited guests, like myself,
sat around the room to observe.

Except for the size of the people in the chairs
and their youthful voices, the role play was remarkably realistic. Those playing parents said
what parents would say and those playing principal and teacher did the same. The girl playing
the victim actually began to cry on cue. Except
for one participant with a minor role who occasionally smiled self-consciously and glanced
at a classmate in the audience, everyone played
his or her role to the hilt. As often happens in

role plays, the imaginary event began to feel real and the actors became their characters. I found myself feeling quite moved.

The class discussion after the role play ended was also remarkable. The students immediately identified the same key questions that a group of adults would address. Is punishment effective? Would this kind of emotional event be more likely to change hurtful behavior? Would this help the victim?

The guidance counselor told me after the conference that the boy who played the father of the victimized sixth-grade girl in the role play often plays the role of the bully and the tease in real life. She felt that having him take the role of a caring father whose daughter was victimized would help him gain some insight into the impact of his own hurtful behavior and empathy for his victims. I do not know whether it changed his behavior.

Truancy

Conferencing can also be used for school offenses that are victimless, such as truancy. Parents and others who have been affected by the young person's behavior are informally the victims in the conference.

Joan was sent to an alternative school by her probation officer when she returned home after completing a residential drug-and-alcohol treatment program. Her attendance was satisfactory for a short time, then she missed more and more school. Having exhausted all the usual strategies to encourage attendance, Joan's program counselor asked another counselor to organize a restorative conference, since he felt too frustrated with his counselee to facilitate the conference himself.

The facilitator invited Joan's mother and father, her probation officer and, of course, the counselor who initiated the conference. When she asked who should act as a support, Joan wanted to bring her friend Eva, with whom she probably used drugs on the days she missed school. The facilitator hesitated, wondering how Eva might influence the conference, but she decided to go along with Joan's request.

The conference was emotional. Joan's parents were in tears and her father told her how frightened he was each time the program counselor called him at work to say that his daughter had not arrived at school. He would imagine finding her overdosed and dead. Everyone agreed that missing school was a clear indicator that she was using drugs again. Her probation officer said that he could not allow Joan to continue violating her probation and endangering herself. He was considering a long-term residential treatment placement.

Eva seemed to impact Joan most, perhaps because it was most unexpected. She cried and told Joan that she was her best friend and she didn't want Joan to go away again. Eva pointed out what Joan needed to do to straighten out her life, although Eva probably should have been heeding her own advice.

In the agreement phase of the conference, Joan apologized to her parents, counselor and probation officer for all the problems and heartache she had caused. She agreed to attend Narcotics Anonymous meetings every day and to record an entry about each meeting in her journal. She also promised not to miss anymore days of school. Even if she didn't feel well, she would at least report to school and find someone to give her a ride home if she still felt sick. All the adults were satisfied with the conference and were particularly pleased with the friend's contribution.

The participation of peers who are also getting in trouble can be appropriate in a conference. I have heard (but don't know details) of conferences where fellow gang members attended and made a positive contribution. The conference facilitator needs to make a judgment call whether to include potentially negative peers and should talk to the proposed support persons before allowing their participation.

In this case Joan followed through with her commitments. At first she would write only a sentence or two in her journal about the N.A. meetings she attended. Then she started to note

what people said at the meetings in greater de-
tail, but never said anything about herself. Several weeks into her journal writing she began to
proudly report that she spoke at the meeting and
record what she had said. Her attendance was
impeccable. She finished the school year with
flying colors.

Not all conferences go as well as Joan's. In
a rather imperfect conference for a boy who
was truant, the facilitator allowed the adults to
dominate the agreement phase. She should have
checked each proposed item in the agreement
with the offender, asking him if he agreed before
allowing any other suggestions. Instead she let
the adults draw up the list and when it was completed, turned to the offender and asked him if
he agreed. He got up without saying a word and
left the building.

The conference facilitator realized that she
had not run the conference properly. She apologized for her mistake, but did not know what to
do about it.

Surprisingly, the next day the boy came to
school. And the next. And the next. Something in
the conference had affected him and he attended
school regularly.

In still another seemingly imperfect truancy
conference a friend of mine ran, he couldn't
get anyone to say more than a few words. Jose
lived with his grandmother, who came to the

conference, and when the facilitator asked the grandmother how she had been affected by her grandson's truancy, she looked at her grandson sternly and said, "He knows how I feel." A fellow student and Jose's school counselor had only a little to say, appearing constrained by the tone the grandmother had set. The agreement was simply that Jose would attend school. The whole conference lasted about 20 minutes.

The facilitator blamed himself for what he felt was a disastrous event. He speculated whether he should have spent a lot more time with the grandmother beforehand so she would have been more comfortable. His concerns were unwarranted. Jose began attending school every day. Despite the brevity of the conference and the apparent lack of free expression of emotion, that one look and few words from his grandmother evidently spoke volumes to Jose.

Certainly there have been many truancy conferences that did not produce such sterling results. Conferences are not a panacea but they can have a significant impact on a great many kids.

In Minnesota truancy is defined as seven unexcused absences. At that point it becomes a legal matter and is referred to juvenile probation. In Rice County, Minnesota, about 40 miles south of Minneapolis-St. Paul, the local junior high school intervened with a restorative conference,

facilitated by the police officer assigned to that
building, after the third unexcused absence. With
an enrollment of about a thousand students,
the junior high had between 30 and 40 truants
each year for a five-year period. The year they
introduced systematic use of conferencing the
number of truants fell to five.

School conferencing is of special value to paro-
chial and other private schools whose reputations
are critical to attracting tuition-paying students.
Part of the incentive for parents to send their
children to private institutions is that they are
supposed to be safer, sheltered from the drugs,
violence and other issues that plague many
public schools. When incidents do arise, private
school administrators may often find themselves
conflicted about what to do. React harshly and
purge the menace? Sweep it under the carpet?
Risk publicity and a loss of students? Risk an-
tagonizing parents and alumni? Conferencing
addresses the offense squarely, but in a way that
parents and others are almost always satisfied
with the outcome.

Conferencing is a promising response to behavior problems in schools, but it will require a
change of mind-set and philosophy among some
school administrators. A friend of mine was telling an assistant principal at a junior high school
about conferencing. The administrator reacted
with dismay. He said that all he had to do was

look in his school district's disciplinary handbook to see what punishment was prescribed for the student's offense and then see that it was carried out. Why would he want to get involved with this conferencing stuff?

Some administrators are not only unwilling to be inconvenienced by such a process, but they are also not going to let anyone else do it. In one instance, a school administrator interfered in an appropriately authorized conference by expelling several of the students who had committed the offense before the conference was held, but allowed others to participate in the conference. This cast a dark shadow on the subsequent conference and created a legal hassle about the uneven treatment of the offenders. Despite evidence that harsh punishment neither serves students nor improves behavior in schools, there are those who are simply stuck in ineffective ways. They would rather go down with the old ship than consider traveling on a new vessel.

13

Campus

Conferences have been held on college and university campuses. Because most college students are adults under the law, parental involvement would occur only if the offender requested it. Nonetheless, "campus conferencing" is the same process—except an offending student might have roommates or other friends there for support if he or she did not want to include parents or other relatives.

Institutions of higher learning face the same issues as the rest of society: more inappropriate behavior, more crime, more violence and a notable lack of success in dealing with it. For colleges and universities, conferencing offers a meaning-

ful way to address offenses with less risk of losing
tuition-paying students or offending alumni. The
college administrator or resident assistant could
deal with a wide range of problems by involving
those who have been affected and letting them
decide the outcome.

Drug Overdose

Lon, a young man at a small college, overdosed on drugs and had to be rushed to the
local hospital where he recovered. Lon and his
brother both attended the school and neither
had previous disciplinary violations. The college administration did not want to ignore this
serious incident so they convened a restorative
conference.

Lon readily admitted the stupidity of what he
did. He said that taking drugs was not typical
behavior for him.

Two key "victims" in this offense were the
campus security officer and the school nurse
who were both responsible for responding to
the emergency. The officer told the youth how
disturbed he had felt to find someone in such a
life-threatening situation, and the school nurse
shared how frightened she was that Lon might
die. Lon was very moved by their sincere concern
for his well-being, and recognized that he had
put them through an ordeal. He agreed to avoid
such behavior in the future and, as part of the

outcome, committed himself to a defined amount of community service work.

At the close of the conference Lon thanked everyone, including the conference facilitator, for addressing the incident with a conference. He said that by having a chance to talk with everyone, he felt less embarrassed. He had feared that he would spend the next couple of years on campus seeing people who had been involved and feeling that they would look at him as a "druggie" because of what he did. Although he had been very nervous about the conference, he felt much better now that he had attended.

Team Conference

Another area of campus life where wrongdoing needs to be addressed more effectively is in sports. Inappropriate behavior is sometimes ignored because punishment has consequences for the whole team. Conferencing is an alternate response that heals rather than disrupts.

Recently a friend of mine ran a conference for a college sports team torn by internal strife. Don, an excessively competitive student, had repeatedly antagonized his teammates. After Rick, the team captain, overheard him complaining about his teammates to a professor, the entire team stopped talking to Don.

Dissension poisoned the team's morale. The coach unsuccessfully tried to resolve the conflict,

but after weeks of frustration he turned the issues over to a conference facilitator.

Don reluctantly agreed to the conference. The
facilitator encouraged him to take responsibility
for his behavior. As the conference began, Don
apologized to his teammates for his negative
behavior. He explained that his parents were
getting divorced, his girlfriend had dropped
him and his best friend just died. He accepted
responsibility. With deep emotion, he asked his
teammates to forgive him for his rude and inappropriate behavior.

Each team member had an opportunity to tell
Don how his behavior had affected them personally and how he had disrupted team unity. Rick,
however, refused to give up his anger and accept
Don's apology. The rest of the team confronted
Rick's stubbornness. A freshman expressed how
disappointed he was in the captain's reaction,
how he and the younger team members looked
up to Rick as a role model.

Negative feelings resonated for some time with
the conference providing a safe environment for
the exchange of emotion. Gradually the focus
shifted toward how to repair the harm. The team
defined a plan for resolution of the issues and
everyone, including Don and Rick, agreed to work
together. By the end of the conference a feeling of
cooperation and camaraderie had been restored.
The coach, who invited my friend to facilitate the

conference, was thrilled with the outcome and has since become an advocate of conferencing.

Campus crime, misconduct and other inappropriate behavior, as in the rest of society, is generally handled with little regard for the emotions of all involved. By defining the appropriate offenses for conferences with the local police and public prosecutor and institutional authorities, and then systematically using conferencing, many perplexing and destructive incidents could be handled constructively, satisfying victims, offenders and everyone who cares about them.

14

Court

The first conference I ever attended was for the arson incident described in Chapter 6, conducted under the auspices of a juvenile court. The two youths who had committed the offense had already been adjudicated and were in a detention center, awaiting placement in a long-term residential treatment facility. The conference was not diversionary, that is, it was not an alternative to juvenile court or school disciplinary procedures. Rather, it was a supplement to the existing court process and was intended to provide healing and closure for the victims, the offenders, their friends and families, and the community.

Diverting an Assault

Courts can still divert cases after police referral. Usually a probation officer has discretion at the point of intake into the juvenile probation system or even afterward, when a probation officer is assigned the case. For example, a probation officer who had been assigned a male youth charged with assault decided to handle the case as a restorative conference. As the facilitator began contacting everyone in preparation for the conference, he realized that the probation officer had made a wise decision in diverting the case from court.

The offender, Alex, hit a smaller boy, David, at his high school. When the facilitator called Alex, the youth sounded confused and defensive. He was confused because months had passed since charges had been filed. Having no experience with police or courts, he assumed that the matter had been dropped. He was defensive because he blamed David for the incident. He explained that David had harassed him all afternoon, emptying a pencil sharpener full of shavings over his head near the end of class period. As they left the classroom, David continued to pursue him down the hall. Alex lost his temper and hit the smaller boy, who fell and hurt his head.

Alex, who was a good student and athlete, had been shocked to find himself suspended from high school for several days and charged with assault. He said that he was willing to participate in the conference, especially since it was his only alternative to going to juvenile court, but he still seemed to blame David for the incident. When the facilitator called David's home his mother was irate. She felt that Alex should be punished by the courts and was not happy about the restorative conference. When the facilitator explained the advantages of the conference—that she would a get a chance to say how she felt directly to Alex— she eventually agreed, if her son would want to participate.

In his phone conversation with David, the facilitator learned that Alex had been accurate in describing the events that preceded the assault. Admitting his harassing behavior, David insisted that Alex should not have hit him and was willing to participate in the conference.

The facilitator decided to visit Alex and his parents at their home. He knew that David's mother's moral indignation and anger would skyrocket if Alex tried to blame her son. He spent almost an hour encouraging Alex to take responsibility for the assault, even if he felt he was provoked by David. At some point Alex began to realize that he had responded to the other youth's annoying behavior by hitting him, even though he had other choices. So the responsibility for the assault was his, not David's. At the conference David's mother was still irate, even though the offender admitted his responsibility at the outset. She said that her family would never have pressed charges if Alex had at least apologized. Alex claimed that he did apologize, the very next day. The victim's mother looked at her son who hung his head and said, "I forgot to tell you." From that point on the conference went rather smoothly toward resolution, bringing to a satisfactory conclusion an incident that did not belong in the criminal justice system.

Coma Conference

The next conference was unusual. It was held in the home of a victim who was in a coma and did not follow the conference script. Even though this was not a normal conference, the outcome was so positive that I feel compelled to include it in this book.

Ken and Tony had been drinking and doing drugs. Ken, who was driving that night, lost control and wrecked the car. Tony, in the passenger seat, was almost killed and remained in a coma. Tony's mother Rita devoted herself to caring for her son at home. Two years after the tragedy the probation officer in the case arranged for a restorative conference at Tony's home. Rita wanted the conference at home so Ken could see her son. Ken had not visited Tony since the car crash.

The conference began with a startling occurrence. When Ken entered the house, accompanied by the probation officer and the conference facilitator, he went to Tony's bedside. Tony abruptly sat up with a loud gasp and then fell back onto his bed, remaining in a coma. Rita explained that the doctor had warned her that, even in a coma, sometimes an individual may react strongly to the sound of a familiar voice.

The conference was held near the bed of the unconscious victim. The facilitator immediately abandoned the script, recognizing that Rita and Ken had known each other for years and their discussion needed little facilitation. Rita began the conference by telling Ken she didn't know whether to tear his head off or hug him. She acknowledged that if Tony had been driving, Ken might easily have been the person in the coma. But she couldn't understand why Ken hadn't come to visit. Ken apologized and explained that he'd been afraid to visit, fearful that Rita wouldn't want to see him because of what he had done to Tony.

As the intensity of the exchange subsided, the facilitator raised the issue of the conference agreement. Rita wanted Ken to commit himself to a long-term drug-and-alcohol treatment program and make a promise to visit regularly. Ken readily agreed. As a result of the conference, a tremendous emotional burden for two unhappy individuals was cast off and replaced by a mutually supportive relationship.

Several months after the conference Rita said that her only regret about the conference was that it did not occur sooner. Ken successfully completed substance-abuse treatment and Ken's and Rita's families had Easter dinner together.

Sex Offender

A conference can help reintegrate an offender into his family and his community. A probation officer facilitated a conference for Jerry, an adolescent offender who had spent two years in a sexual-offender treatment program after repeatedly fondling and, on one occasion, having sexual intercourse with his sister's little girl while serving as her babysitter. Other adult siblings of Jerry and his sister, none of whom lived locally, had criticized Jerry's sister for involving the police, perhaps not knowing the details of the offense and equating the sexual abuse with children "playing doctor."

Jerry's sister and her husband were at the conference but did not want their daughter present. Instead they read a letter their daughter had written to her Uncle Jerry. The offender took responsibility for what he had done and achieved some degree of reconciliation with his sister and brother-in-law. Most significantly, Jerry agreed to contact their brothers and sisters and advise them that what he had done was very serious and warranted involving the police.

That outcome was of great value to his sister who had been inappropriately criticized by her own family.

Check Forger

I have heard some probation officers protest that they should not run conferences for their own clients. There are some advantages to doing so. A probation officer facilitated a conference for Ron who, while on probation, forged some of his mother's checks.

Ron started the conference by apologizing. His mother was irate but often interrupted her anger with a joke. A frown appeared on Ron's face whenever she did this.

The stepfather talked about his disappointment. He said that he had a good relationship with Ron but now felt betrayed and didn't know how his trust would be restored.

As the conference proceeded the mother and her son bickered until, in an outburst of rage, Ron shouted at his mother to stop joking around, telling her he hated how she made everything into a joke.

A little later in the conference one of the girls who came to support Ron talked about how he and his mother reminded her of her relationship with her mother. She said that she and her mother loved each other but always fought until they went to family counseling. Now they get along a lot better. She wondered if Ron and his mother would be willing to go to counseling.

Both Ron and his mother said that they would be willing, but the mother was concerned about the cost. Because the probation officer was facilitating the conference, he was there to assure them that the court would be willing to pay for counseling sessions if both of them agreed to attend regularly. So the counseling was built into the conference agreement.

The conference had a positive effect on Ron. He kept his commitments, attended the counseling sessions faithfully and improved his relationship with his mother and stepfather. He even improved his school attendance and grades, although those issues were not addressed in the agreement.

Intolerant Probation Officer

Even when probation officers delegate the conferencing responsibility to others, probation officers still must be trained in conferencing and understand the conference dynamics so that they can appropriately support the process. Otherwise they can cause problems, as happened in a shoplifting conference facilitated by a counselor for the local juvenile probation department.

Barbara, the woman who owned the store, was enraged. Her store had suffered a lot of merchandise loss over the previous year. She believed that the offender, a young girl, had stolen from her many times. She welcomed the opportunity to vent her feelings at the offender.

But once the conference was convened, Barbara realized that the youth had not lived in the community long enough to be part of her long-term problem. Also the youth was extremely apologetic and willing to take responsibility for what she had done.

As is often the case, a victim who displays strong emotions can swing from intense negative feelings to intense positive feelings. In the agreement phase of the conference Barbara was remarkably generous and compassionate to the offender, who had suffered personal problems.

After the conference Barbara told the conference facilitator that if she could ever help the offender, she would. The probation officer who had seen Barbara's preconference anger was annoyed by her extreme emotional turnabout and showed her disapproving look on her face. Barbara recognized the disapproval and burst into tearful shame and anger. She was revictimized by the probation officer's ignorant intolerance. Whether or not probation officers facilitate the conference, they should be trained to understand that such swings of emotion are commonplace among victims in conferences.

In some communities conferencing has been initiated as a collaboration with other local agencies. In Bucks County, Pennsylvania, for example,

juvenile probation officers may refer cases, before
or after adjudication, to be conferenced by a pool
of volunteers who are recruited and trained under
the auspices of the local victim services agency.
In Minneapolis, several community organizations
are collaborating with the local courts and police
by recruiting and training qualified volunteers to
conference neighborhood crimes such as pros-
titution, drug-dealing and other street crimes
that foster the deterioration of neighborhoods.
Conferencing not only has the potential to change
the way the courts deal with crime, but also to
involve the public in a meaningful role as well.

15

Corrections

The least developed but potentially one of the most valuable uses of conferencing is in corrections. Prisons and the parole system are ripe for innovation because, as currently constituted, they do not work. The notion of rehabilitation in our correctional institutions is largely a myth.

Prison life is about survival. Few prisoners reflect on their wrongs and feel remorse for what they have done to their victims. The environment of prison is so harsh that prisoners largely see themselves as victims and spend little time thinking about the true victims of their crimes.

Conference Role Play in Prison

When Terry O'Connell was visiting the United
States, we convened a role play of a restorative
conference in Graterford Prison, a large maxi-
mum security facility in Pennsylvania, with the
cooperation of two inmates serving life terms—
Ali Thurman Bonner (to whose memory I have
dedicated this book) and Simon Khaadim Ahad
Evans. These two inmates founded the "School
of Hard Knocks," which provided a life-skills
program to prepare young inmates to successfully stay out of prison, and another program
for troubled youths who visited the prison. They
were excited by conferencing and believed that it
had important implications for preventing crime
and violence among youths. The role play dealt
with Jay, who was serving a five-year sentence for
shooting another youth in a dispute over the right
to sell drugs on a street corner in Philadelphia.
We asked a police officer who had recently been
trained in conferencing to facilitate the conference. Terry, my wife Susan and several inmates
volunteered to play the victim, the victim's relatives and Jay's relatives. Lacking women for all
the female roles, I played the offender's mother.
Jay participated in the conference as himself.

The role play may sound comical, but it was
not. The conference was imaginary, but the shooting had been very real. Within minutes everyone
was quite serious and immersed in their roles.

We had no difficulty imagining the anger and disgust we would feel if someone hurt a member of our family, nor our shame if our son or brother were arrested for harming someone else. The role play was a powerful emotional experience for all of us.

Even though Jay had served three years of his sentence, he had never thought about all the implications of his crime. Ali later reported that Jay spent a couple of tearful hours on the telephone, apologizing to his mother for the harm he had done to his family.

In a video interview Jay said, "With the family conference, I realized that I hurt so many people. I didn't just hurt the victim. I hurt my family members, people around me, everybody that's got to deal with me and I got to deal with them. I hurt everybody. I hurt a lot of people."

Although I have some difficulty imagining spending three years in prison without realizing the harm I had done to my family, I am not Jay and have not had to walk in his shoes. Clearly restorative conferencing touched him and made him more empathetic than he had been before. Imagine what the real conference might have accomplished.

We have secured the cooperation of interested state and local corrections officials who want to experiment with conferencing for both juvenile and adult offenders. In addition to the possibility of inmates experiencing conferences with actual victims or in conference role plays, we also envision using conferencing as a response to probation and parole violations. Rather than automatically returning an offender to a prison or juvenile detention center, depending on the violation, conferences may allow the offender to face the violation squarely, experience the emotional consequences, make amends and take steps to remedy any harm that resulted. Too often an offender is returned to confinement when a meaningful interim step may be more appropriate.

Disciplinary incidents in prisons and detention centers also present opportunities for worthwhile conferences. Disciplining inmates for breaking rules or for offenses against other inmates or staff does not resolve the feelings that caused or resulted from the incident. A conference gets at the roots of the conflict and reduces the chance for a recurrence.

Each incident that is conferenced presents another opportunity for inmates to see the real consequences of their impulsive behavior. Punishment, on the other hand, gives inmates another opportunity to see themselves as victims and make excuses for what they have done. Many inmates go through their entire lives without ever really looking at themselves, because their homes, schools and communities have always responded with stigmatizing punishment that allowed them to be passive and resent authority. Conferencing holds offenders accountable in that they have to talk and think and experience other people's feelings.

Unlike with school, police and court conferencing, there has been little experience with corrections conferencing. Given the impact of conferencing with offenders in other settings, however, there is good reason to expect that conferences in correctional institutions and the probation and parole system will prove worthwhile. Even if re-offense rates do not decline, the value to victims who want to face offenders is reason enough. We have to keep reminding ourselves that conferencing is, first and foremost, a service that we can offer to victims.

Returning from the Institution

The teen-age victim, Colin, had been involved in a fight with four other youths when the police intervened. Although the youth seemed to have no serious injuries, that night he experienced convulsions and fell into a coma. The four offenders were arrested and the juvenile court judge sent them all to residential treatment facilities for at least six months, after which their cases would be reviewed. In the meantime Colin emerged from the coma, but had suffered physical impairment to his motor functions and speech.

During the six months the four offenders were away the probation officer visited Colin and his family. The youth had experienced some physical improvement through intensive rehabilitation, but he and his family were filled with anger. Colin openly talked about revenge, promising to find each of the offenders when they returned to the community and get back at them, one at a time. The probation officer, recognizing that this family desperately needed a way to get some resolution and move beyond their anger, suggested the possibility of a restorative conference. Although Colin dismissed the idea at the time, the probation officer felt that he had given the victim and his family something to think about.

When the six months had elapsed, the four youths were escorted back to the juvenile court by counselors from the residential institutions. Colin and his family also attended the review hearing. The judge decided that the four offenders would be reassigned from secure treatment to foster homes closer to their home communities.

The probation officer decided to use the opportunity provided by the court hearing, which had brought everyone together, to again offer a restorative conference. Having had several months to think about the conference idea, Colin and his parents now expressed interest in participating. The offenders agreed as well. Although the offenders' parents were not at the hearing, the probation officer asked the residential counselors to serve as their supports in the conference.

In a small room, the only one available, the probation officer assembled the conference. Following the script, the conference provided an opportunity for everyone to talk, unlike the review hearing that just proceeded it. Colin had played no role in the review hearing. Also, he had been in the hospital when the offenders went through their initial court hearing. This was the first time that the offenders had seen Colin since the assault.

As Colin walked and spoke and gestured, his impaired functions were starkly demonstrated. The four offenders began to realize the damage they had done to another human being. One of them began to cry. Feelings are contagious and soon all four offenders offered tearful apologies to the injured boy and his parents. Colin and his parents, moved by the sincerity of the four youths, readily offered their forgiveness.

The probation officer watched in amazement as the conference process worked its magic. The four offenders, long detached from the reality of their crime, faced what they had done and repented. Colin, until now obsessed with thoughts of revenge, and his parents freed themselves from anger and put closure on a horrible episode in their lives.

Rape and Murder

Ironically, the most compelling examples of the good that can result from face-to-face encounters between victims and offenders have been carried out with the most heinous crimes. I recently spent four gut-wrenching days at a training in which I heard from a panel of families of murder victims, visited a prison to hear from a panel of men convicted of murder, and watched hours of videotape of meetings between families of murder victims and murderers.

While we may recoil from the idea of ever facing the monsters who could do such horrible things to us or people we love, after seeing the videotapes I have no doubt that for many victims and their families the benefits are critical. For those who choose to proceed, the opportunity to express feelings directly to the offender and to ask questions can provide healing. One father of a murdered child, who was at our training all four days, assured us that meeting his daughter's killers was a critical step in putting some closure on the worst experience of his life.

Another father told us how the man who raped and murdered his child, after being convicted, turned toward the victim's family on his way out of the courtroom and gestured at them with his middle finger. Obviously that father and his family have absolutely no interest in meeting with such a lunatic.

But where the offender is willing to meet, to answer questions, to express remorse, even if he does not take full responsibility for his actions, families can begin to reconstruct the story of their lives. People who experience violent crimes have had the fabric of their life torn apart. They need to get answers to mend their understanding. Why me? Or why my loved one? They need to know details. How did she die? Did she suffer? What did she say? What did you say? What did you do? They want the truth.

Many of their questions can be answered only by the offender and the process may take many hours. Strangely, they and the offender have the offense as a common bond. Talking and questioning and expressing feelings seems to bring the victim or the victim's family to a point where they can finally begin weaving new sections in their life story, whereas before the meeting they were endlessly stuck in trying to patch holes that could never be mended.

The offenders also gain from the encounter. Many of them committed violent crimes in fits of anger or while using alcohol or drugs, which allowed them to do things that they might never have done when they were sober. The offenders who agree to participate seem to do so out of a genuine interest in helping the victims or the victims' surviving family and friends. But sometimes they gain forgiveness as well.

I left the training emotionally drained, but in absolute awe of the resilience of the human spirit. And I realized that isolating offenders and victims as we do, making such encounters the exception rather than the rule, is a terrible mistake.

To date, victim-offender mediators have been the pioneers in bringing serious offenders together with their victims or victims' families. But I trust that conferences will soon occur, probably involving more family members and close friends of the victims and offenders than the victim-offender mediations. Conferences involving severe offenses will require substantial preparation and will not occur until at least several years after the crime.

Most offenders will emerge from prison into our society with less understanding and compassion than when they entered. Most victims will struggle with their anger and their fear much longer than necessary, and in some cases indefinitely. Not everyone will choose to participate in conferences for serious offenses, but for those who are interested and willing, we ought to offer them an opportunity for real justice.

16

Workplace

Samantha, just out of college, had a noisy party at her apartment. Without her knowledge, a young man who was one year younger than the legal drinking age was among the many guests. When a police officer stopped to tell the group to quiet down, he also randomly checked the identification of some of the guests and discovered the young man drinking alcoholic beverages. Besides charging the underage guest, he also charged the hostess with "corrupting the morals of a minor." When Samantha expressed fear that such a charge threatened her job as a counselor at a program for delinquent youths, the police officer assured her that the charge was routine and that the public prosecutor would treat the matter lightly.

The police officer was wrong. When Samantha went to the initial hearing without an attorney, she realized that the matter was being taken very seriously. Although the criminal charge jeopardized her position as a youth counselor, she said nothing to her work supervisors during the months the wheels of justice slowly turned, although she had many opportunities. Everyone at work found out about her troubles when her name and the offense appeared in the newspaper.

The program director phoned Samantha to explain that "corrupting the morals of a minor," unless extenuating circumstances were thoroughly justified and documented, were usually grounds for automatic dismissal from her job. Further, she had undermined her supervisors' trust by keeping the offense secret for months. He asked if she would be willing to handle the situation with a workplace conference and explained what that meant. He said that he did not have the same emotional reaction to the situation as her direct supervisors and felt he could appropriately facilitate the conference. She agreed to the conference, not entirely sure what the alternative would have been.

At the conference the next day Samantha apologized profusely. Both supervisors told her bluntly how foolish she had been. Not only could they have guided her to a good attorney, but also they and her coworkers could have provided emotional support. They both felt they had a friendly and mutually respectful relationship with her and were shocked and hurt that she had kept the truth from them, particularly for such a long time. Her coworker whom she had nominated as her support agreed that it was tough, but he also admitted feeling badly that she had not trusted him enough to share her problems.

Samantha was reduced to tears. She said that she always had a hard time bringing up embarrassing problems and that she realized now she had hurt people who had trusted her.

Samantha profusely apologized to her supervisors. The agreement produced by the conference stated that she would work with her supervisors to address the criminal charge. The program director had arranged for refreshments after the conference and the young woman, her coworker and her supervisors all had an opportunity to talk informally before returning to work. Eventually the charge was dropped and Samantha kept her job.

Instead of convening a conference, the program director could have called the counselor to his office for a verbal reprimand, given her a written reprimand that would also be copied to her personnel file, put her on probationary status or simply fired her. But the conference allowed everyone affected by her poor judgment and lack of trust to deal with their feelings and she could make amends, shed her offender label and begin to repair the harm she had done to her relationships with her supervisors and coworkers.

Wrongdoing and inappropriate behavior in the workplace are usually handled badly. Aside from how the offense or behavior itself is addressed, workplaces rarely respond to the emotional implications of the problem. Morale and productivity are casualties of the unresolved feelings of the offending employee, their coworkers and supervisors. A workplace conference, which provides a forum for everyone who has been affected to express feelings and help shape the outcome, is a far less disruptive approach to addressing employee problems. An employee who has been confronted in a conference is less likely to feel resentful and victimized by the supervisor and more likely to see how he affected others and change his behavior.

Supervision and Evaluation

Sometimes the conferencing process identifies employees who are not willing to accept constructive supervision. Lana, an employee whose inappropriate behavior had raised serious concerns with her supervisors, was offered an opportunity for a workplace conference. Although the conference process was explained in the most supportive terms, the woman decided to quit her job instead. For both the company and the supervisors, Lana's decision to leave was a benefit of the conferencing process.

Conferencing can also be a useful evaluation. Aspects of personality and values may emerge in a conference that cause you to see that person differently, as the following story illustrates.

Louise, a bank loan officer, helped an unemployed friend get a small business loan by knowingly allowing her friend to list her previous job as current employment. Later, the misrepresentation came to light but Louise was a valued employee and bank management decided to handle her offense with a workplace conference.

At the conference, although Louise admitted what she did, she tried to distinguish her offense from taking money from the bank for herself. Even though her supervisors and colleagues acknowledged that it was not as serious as stealing, Louise failed to appreciate that her offense was significant and to show evidence of regret. She kept saying her friend had repaid the loan and that she herself derived no financial gain from the transaction.

The loan officer was not fired. She was demoted to less independent status in making loans. Significantly, she was no longer perceived as a candidate for promotion to management. Had she responded appropriately her offense would have been viewed as a lapse in an otherwise commendable career. Through the conference, however, she had demonstrated a character flaw that precluded further advancement at that bank.

Complex Dispute

Sometimes workplace conferencing is confused with mediation or other conflict resolution strategies, but conferencing is a deliberately emotional strategy. The script, with its open-ended questions, repeatedly asks participants how they were affected. Although we perceive ourselves as creatures of reason, our feelings are the key to resolution of conflict.

Harry had always been in conflict with his coworkers. He wanted to return to his job in a heavy industrial plant after a long disability leave, but found the company unwilling to have him back. The union supported Harry, but his immediate coworkers, who were also union members, supported the company's position. The complex dispute had dragged on more than a year when the company and the union agreed to allow a workplace conference facilitator to try to break the impasse.

Without a singular incident or clear admission of wrongdoing, the case was not one that would typically be handled as a workplace conference, but the conference facilitator was satisfied that Harry was willing to admit that he could be nasty and argumentative. He convened the conference on that basis.

The conference was tumultuous. The workers, union and company representatives did not respectfully wait for each person to finish speaking. They interrupted and shouted. The facilitator kept the conference within boundaries, but they were broader boundaries than usual.

Harry admitted that he could be an "S.O.B." Some of the coworkers reminded him of fights he had provoked. Other coworkers were willing to admit acts of revenge, like nailing Harry's boots to the floor of the locker room. But after an hour of loud argument the issue of what to do about Harry was still not resolved.

Among Harry's supporters at the conference was his sister. When the facilitator asked how she was affected by Harry's negative behavior, she acknowledged Harry could be a difficult person. But then she proceeded to tell the entire group the story of their childhood, of their violent, drunken father and his rampages, of Harry's courage in protecting his siblings, of the night her father broke a chair over Harry's back when he defended the family against his violence. There wasn't a dry eye at the conference. A whole new perception of Harry emerged and a new understanding of why he was such a difficult person.

Harry himself was so choked with emotion that the facilitator adjourned the conference.

He and his sister went out for a breath of air.
By the time they returned, the company and the
union had reached an agreement. Although Harry
would not return to work, the company made a
cash settlement in the form of a trust fund that
would pay him a regular stipend in addition to
his existing pension benefits.

Everyone agreed that this was an equitable
way to resolve the dispute. After more than a
year of wrangling between company and union
representatives and their respective attorneys,
the free flow of human emotion washed away
the two parties' differences and a settlement was
achieved.

Human beings are creatures of emotion.

Family Business

In another conference, two principals in a
family business came together to confront differences that had simmered for a long time.
Each party had unresolved feelings toward the
other that had affected the company. Employees
had taken sides with one owner over the other.
Snide comments were being muttered under
people's breath. Mocking looks were exchanged
when backs were turned. In short, the company
was becoming an unhealthy and conflict-ridden
place to work. A third owner, also a member of
the family, convinced the two feuding owners to
participate in a workplace conference.

The facilitator tried to get each party to take some responsibility for his own behavior, but neither was ready to make a clear-cut admission. So she brought them together and asked each of them questions about how the other person's actions had affected them. On one occasion the conference broke down when one of the owners stormed out of the room. At that point, in private conversation, the facilitator cautioned the individual who left that unless he and his co-owner settled their issues and reversed the negative environment they had created in their company, there wasn't going to be a company in a couple of years. The owner returned to the conference.

The intense exchange of emotion that occurred in the safety of the conference allowed issues to be aired. Many issues were based on erroneous assumptions about the other individual, which, when brought to light, proved to be misunderstandings. As the free exchange continued the emotion moved from negative to positive. The two owners soon developed a plan for repairing the harm they had caused by their inappropriate behavior, including informing their employees that the feud had ended.

Conferencing has been around for less than a decade, while workplace conferencing is still in its infancy. Anyone who has experienced the power of the process recognizes that it will change the way we do business.

17

Avoiding Surprises

A facilitator, in preparing for the conference, tries to avoid surprises. The more one anticipates the issues that might arise, the better the conference is likely to be. Learning the details of the incident, talking with all the participants, building rapport, hearing what they think and feel, making personal visits whenever one feels that the victim or offender would benefit—those efforts can prevent unexpected problems in the conference.

Uncooperative Victim

Nonetheless, surprises happen. In the very first conference that I facilitated at an alternative school Roberto, the victim, surprised me. He had been threatened by Eddie, who was angry because Roberto had been allowed to play his choice of music in an activity period at the school. Despite the triviality of the dispute, Eddie ran out to the school van that transported Roberto and pounded on the van windows as the vehicle pulled away. The van driver reported that Eddie screamed and threatened that he would get the victim the next day.

The alternative school decided to discharge Eddie, whose behavior was spiraling downward, unless he agreed to a conference. In my pre-conference discussion with Roberto, the victim said he wanted to confront Eddie but in the actual conference Roberto suddenly minimized the threats that had been made. One of Roberto's friends, there as a support person, was shocked. When he was asked how the incident affected him, he said that he thought it was very serious and was surprised that Roberto now made light of the threats. The victim's sudden change of heart undermined the effectiveness of the conference.

Eddie refused to offer an apology to Roberto as suggested by his family and friends. He claimed that he didn't do anything wrong. No one could persuade him otherwise and Roberto didn't even try. At that point I realized that Eddie was not even meeting the conference prerequisite of ac-knowledging that he had committed an offense,

so I announced that I was ending the conference. Eddie was startled by my decision and
stormed out into the hallway. Two students who
came as his supporters asked if I would continue
the conference if they could get Eddie to admit his
wrongdoing. I agreed. They returned with a much
more compliant Eddie who apologized and coop-
erated throughout the rest of the conference.

When I gave Roberto a ride home after the
conference, I asked him if he was afraid of Eddie
getting back at him. Roberto said that he wasn't
afraid of that, but he had been thinking about all
the crazy things he had done and fights he had
caused when he was on drugs and just didn't feel
right "making a big thing of it" when Eddie did it
to him. We both agreed that Eddie, who had successfully completed a residential drug-and-alcohol treatment program some months before, had
probably relapsed. I asked Roberto if he thought
Eddie had been high during the conference. Roberto agreed that it certainly was possible.

The next day Eddie violated all the commitments he made during the conference. He was
discharged from the school. Obviously conferencing does not always positively influence behavior,
especially when the offender is abusing drugs
and alcohol. Eddie was sent back to a treatment
program by his probation officer.

Conferencing is not a substitute for counseling, for drug-and-alcohol treatment or for

other kinds of interventions and assessments. Rather, it is a narrowly defined way to replace arbitrary punishment for wrongdoing. That's all. The conference outcome is determined by the participants. Other recommendations or actions that professionals might propose for the offender are not the business of the conference. The participants may propose some of those same conditions for the offender. If the offender agrees and if there is funding available, then they may happen, but that is incidental to the primary purpose—for the offender and other conference participants to agree on how to remedy the harm that was done.

Other Offenses

On other occasions, as mentioned in an earlier story, other crimes may be reported by the offender. If the group is shocked or distracted by the offense, then the conference should be stopped. But if the offender is merely trying to "come clean" about other relatively minor offenses, like an old incident of shoplifting, the conference should proceed. If the offense that is mentioned warrants further attention, but not in the current conference, the facilitator may talk to the offender afterward. The offender is protected by the confidentiality of the conference, so the facilitator can only encourage a voluntary action on the part of the offender.

Routine Conference

Even a seemingly routine conference can surprise the facilitator. Two young boys, Paul and Steve, went into the home of a neighbor whose door was ajar and stole loose change. A neighbor saw the boys go into the house and told the boys' parents. Both sets of parents confronted their sons, who readily admitted the offense. The parents were extremely upset with their sons' behavior. Before they called the neighbors who were the victims, they called the local police to ask if an officer could give their children a lecture or something that would make an impression on the boys. The police officer told the parents that rather than a lecture, he would recommend a restorative conference if the victims were willing to participate. The couple whose home had been entered understood that these were only young boys who had taken some loose change. But they also appreciated that Paul's and Steve's parents wanted to appropriately set limits with their children and agreed to participate.

The conference was proceeding smoothly. The boys were completely remorseful. The parents could not have been more supportive of the victims. The victims could not have been more understanding or generous.

Then Paul, in a true act of contrition, said, "I'm really sorry about the pictures."

The pictures? The facilitator looked at the parents. What pictures? He looked at the victim couple who at first were puzzled, then concerned. He announced a "time out" in the conference and went out into the hall with the couple to talk.

The pictures in question were photos of the wife disrobed in various ways, taken by her husband. They had been hidden in their bedroom dresser. The boys had discovered the pictures, stolen them and showed them to their friends at school.

The facilitator was just as embarrassed as the couple, but when all regained their composure, the couple decided to proceed with the conference. The conference resumed its cooperative tone and reached a satisfactory conclusion. Those of us who plan to facilitate conferences are well reminded that even the most routine conference can produce unexpected twists and turns.

18

Just the Facts

Many readers may remember police sergeant Joe Friday, played by Jack Webb on the long-running television program *Dragnet*. Sergeant Friday advised witnesses to give him "just the facts, ma'am, just the facts." Facts make the criminal justice system run. To prove the case in an adversarial system you must have the right facts. The facts related to a conference are significant to the extent they help the facilitator envision the conference, contact the right people, support the victim and prepare the offender to accept responsibility. Beginning facilitators may focus excessively on the facts. They read the court documentation, but forget that making participants comfortable expressing their feelings is a better use of their energy. Conferences rely more on feelings than facts.

Onlooker at the Assault

Victims often accept even outright lies by offenders if their emotional needs are otherwise met. I facilitated a conference for a serious assault by six youths that occurred in the spring of their senior year at an urban Catholic high school. Ben, a well-intentioned young man in their neighborhood, tried to interest them in doing something more purposeful than drinking beer all evening at their favorite street corner. Not only were they not interested, but they beat him severely until he was rescued by a passerby.

By the time I became involved, about a year after the assault, most of the offenders had been dealt with through the courts. Totally frustrated with the insensitivity of the courts toward her son and her family, Ben's mother asked me if I would facilitate a restorative conference, even though three of the youths had been convicted and placed on probation. Ultimately one of the offenders, Randy, agreed to participate. Another, who had been convicted as an adult and ordered by the judge to participate in the conference, never showed up.

Two days before the conference I realized I had made a serious mistake. I had relied on the facts gathered by the police. Randy had stated he was remorseful for having been present at the assault and not having intervened to stop it. He claimed that he was an onlooker, not a participant. I foolishly assumed that Ben was aware of that police record and had accepted that view. When I mentioned Randy's involvement as an onlooker, Ben objected. He insisted that he distinctly remembered Randy as one of his assailants.

I was in a dilemma. The offender had not admitted the offense, so a key conference prerequisite was not met. Yet Ben wanted to proceed with the conference. I felt that I had to honor the victim. He seemed to fully understand that the only satisfaction he and his supporters might get from the conference was an opportunity to express their feelings. I called Ben's parents, his sister and her boyfriend, and others whom he had nominated as supporters. All were apprised of the less-than-ideal situation. All chose to attend. The morning of the conference I again approached Randy, who arrived at the conference with his father. I strongly suggested that if he had done the assault, this would be a good time and place to admit it, make amends and move on with his life. He was adamant that he did not hit the victim.

The conference began with Randy telling his version of the assault. He apologized for having anything to do with the assault and was willing to accept consequences for his involvement, but he again asserted that he was an onlooker and not a participant.

As he finished speaking Ben challenged him, claiming that he had a clear recollection of those individuals who hit him. Other members of the family expressed their dismay and anger at Randy's resistance to admitting his involvement. When Ben's father referred to the offender as a liar, Randy's father angrily came to his son's defense. That was the only time that I had to intervene in what was a very emotional exchange. I said that it was important that we not call each other names. I reminded everyone that we were here to find out how people have been affected by the incident and how to repair the harm that it caused. Both angry fathers nodded and the conference proceeded emotionally, but without further verbal abuse.

The detective who investigated the assault played an important role in the conference. He was well-regarded by both Ben's and Randy's group. At one point in the conference, he said that Randy's father, when informed of his son's involvement in the assault, immediately asked about the well-being of the victim. This softened the anger of Ben's group.

The detective also supported Ben's version of the assault. He emphasized that he found Ben to be an accurate observer. When he made the initial arrests, even in a street setting with a crowd of teen-agers, he was confident that he was apprehending the correct suspect because of Ben's precise and detailed description of each offender. For that reason, he explained, he was inclined to trust the victim's recollection of who hit him.

Ben's group tried to persuade Randy to recant and admit his involvement in the assault, assuring him that they were not interested in vengeance, just the truth. Given that Randy's version of events differed from Ben's, I was reluctant to limit the discussion and leave the victim and his supporters feeling that they had not had an adequate opportunity to pursue their concerns. The discussion continued for almost an hour.

Suddenly the victim group seemed to shift their mood. Ben and his supporters collectively realized that for over a year Randy had been telling the police and his parents that he was only an onlooker in the assault. If he were lying, as Ben insisted he was, Randy was so deeply invested in his lie that he wasn't going to tell the truth now.

Although Randy would not admit that he hit Ben, he claimed that if he had it to do over again he would have tried to stop the assault or run for help. He agreed that he should have done that when the assault began. He also agreed to do community service as a way of making amends for his involvement. And he apologized.

After the conference Ben told me that he accepted that the offender would never admit the facts of the incident. He said what the conference achieved for him was to put closure on the most traumatic event of his life. However imperfect the conference, it met his underlying emotional needs.

For several centuries and until recently, the evolution of human thought has emphasized intellect and reason. Our culture has disparaged emotion as a weakness, an unpleasant reality that humans should strive to overcome with thoughtfulness and intelligence.

The tide is beginning to turn. We have begun to see the role emotion plays in our lives. Daniel Goleman, longtime science writer for *The New York Times*, said that "emotional intelligence" is a far better predictor of success and well-being than intellectual intelligence. Goleman's landmark book, *Emotional Intelligence*, says our ability to empathize, to understand and appreciate the emotional needs of others, is a key element of emotional intelligence. Conferencing fosters precisely that ability.

Racial Bias

A conference dealing with a high school racial incident highlights the contrast between the current legal system's focus on facts and the Real Justice emphasis on emotion. Two girls were cutting class. They went out to the school parking lot and found an unlocked car in which to smoke cigarettes. They must have known that the car they entered belonged to one of the few African-American students in the school. They wrote the words "Nigger" and "KKK" and drew a Nazi swastika on the upholstery and ceiling of the vehicle. They also burned holes in the seats and the dashboard with their cigarettes and the car's cigarette lighter.

Angel, the girl who owned the car, was devastated. Not only had her car been vandalized, but the racist graffiti made the incident especially painful. The girls were caught and admitted the vandalism. They explained they were only trying to bring attention to the problem of racial bias in their high school. Despite their seemingly ridiculous claim, Angel wanted to handle the offense as a conference rather than wait for it to work slowly through the courts. She wanted to confront the offenders with her feelings and then put the incident behind her. Like the offender in the previously cited assault case, the two girls held to their story, but readily expressed remorse. They agreed to community service work and to publicly apologize to the student body for having brought the negative publicity to the high school and for having offended many students who cared about Angel.

When the girls apologized in the conference, Angel told them that she knew they were not telling the truth about why they vandalized her car. Yet she accepted their apology and acknowledged they were genuinely sorry for what they did.

If we feel frustrated with a conferencing process that tolerates such factual inaccuracies by offenders in the assault and vandalism cases, we might ask ourselves why it's a problem and whose problem it is. If the need for a perfect recitation of the facts gets in the way, why obstruct healing? For victims in both cases, conferencing brought closure and allowed them to move on with their lives.

Passive Offender

I saw a videotape that vividly illustrated this conflict between facts and feelings. The video showed an encounter between one of two offenders and the mother and father of a teen-age girl who was abducted, raped and shot to death. The offender, a dull man apparently easily influenced by the other offender, was remorseful and anxious to make amends. He claimed that the other offender had forced him to participate in the crime at gunpoint, which was probably largely true, especially when the girl was first abducted. The father, who had visited the crime scene, asked the offender why he didn't try to help his daughter or save himself at various intervals that night, particularly when it would have been easy to suddenly run into the thick dark woods.

The offender was unwilling to acknowledge that he had any options.

The father later told those who observed the video that he could not fully accept this offender's story. He was certain that the offender had been more of a participant in the crime than he was willing to admit. The father speculated that the offender could not bring himself to face the truth and may actually believe he played only a passive role. Sadly, I thought, the only one who could have honestly reported the truth was the victim.

The father explained that he and his wife have accepted that the facts of the crime will not be known, that the truth will remain ambiguous. As parents they faced the offenders, voiced their outrage and their grief, gained the understanding they could and then put closure on the greatest tragedy parents can experience. For their own sake and for the well-being of their surviving daughter, they had to address their emotional needs and, like the victims of the assault and the racial incident, try to move on.

Despite Sergeant Friday's assertion, justice is not "just the facts." Our criminal justice system fails to repair the harm caused by crime, because it fails to acknowledge feelings. Justice is not about evidence, proof, witnesses, convictions or punishment. Real justice can be achieved when we address the emotional needs of all who have been affected by a crime.

19

Community

Community is a carelessly used word. We use the word, generally without clarification, to refer to our neighborhood, our region, our colleagues, our world. What we do know about community is that we seem to have lost it. Most of us in the modern world do not feel as connected to others around us as our parents or grandparents did in their time.

Lack of connectedness with others is usually found in young offenders. We should not be surprised. Our society inhibits the development of relationships in many ways.

Families stand alone as supposedly self-sufficient units comprised of a mother, a father and their children. They try to cope with the stresses and struggles of life without the network of extended family that provided mutual support and protection in previous generations.

Half of the nuclear families in the baby-boomer generation broke apart at least once. Children of divorced families often lack trust in the durability of human relationships.

Isolation from extended family often results from our moving from place to place. Some parents' careers demand a move every two or three years. These families may never build lasting relationships with others in their neighborhoods and schools. Many people do not even know their next-door neighbors.

As our institutions grow larger they become more impersonal. After World War II, public schools throughout North America were consolidated into larger administrative units. In the interest of improving school facilities, rural and small-town schools were closed and large regional institutions were created. But what was gained in consolidation was lost in other ways. Many students who now feel alone and adrift in large schools would benefit from the personal attention and camaraderie of a smaller school. That same trend toward bigness and depersonalization is exemplified by the growth of superstores, multinational corporations, big governments and sprawling suburbs.

Government agencies have tried many initiatives to foster a sense of community. But government itself is not community. "Community policing," one of the most widespread initiatives of the criminal justice system, typically involves an administrative decision to create a storefront police substation or shift police from riding in cars to foot patrol or riding on bicycles. The police administration usually does not involve citizens in the decision making or implementation, so there is rarely a sense of connection or ownership that develops. Official efforts that carry the "community" label usually produce superficial results because government sees community as simply part of its geographic jurisdiction.

Defining Community

Community is not a place. Rather, it is a feeling, a perception. When people see themselves as belonging to a community, they feel connected. They have a sense of ownership and responsibility. They feel that they have a say in how things are run and a stake in the outcome. Conferencing creates a sense of ownership and connectedness between people. It can help renew our feeling of community.

The conferencing process fosters involvement and ownership. Conferencing engages people at the outset by asking them to make choices. In preparing for the conference, the

facilitator respectfully invites everyone to participate on a voluntary basis. People have to
decide whether they are willing to attend. Even
offenders, faced with the threat of more formal
disciplinary or legal processes, have a choice.
They can, and sometimes do, refuse to participate in the conference. Again, at the beginning
of the conference, participants are reminded
that participation is their choice. They can leave
at any time.

The conference provides each participant with
an opportunity to speak. Not only is each individual asked a series of open-ended questions,
but the facilitator later checks to see if anyone
has more to say. Most significantly, all of the conference participants have a say in the outcome.
They decide how to repair the harm caused by
the offender. Rarely in our society are individuals
treated with such respect.

The term "micro-community" has been used
to describe the relationship between those who
are brought together in a conference. Initially,
the common bond that the participants share is
the offense. By the end of the process they also
share the experience of the conference itself, an
emotional event that forges relationships between
participants. Long after the conference those
relationships will be quietly acknowledged by a
wave or a knowing smile whenever participants
encounter one another. Police officers have often

told me how an offender from a conference they facilitated now waves when they see each other on the streets.

Government Interference

Some government officials, confusing the concept of community with their own geographic jurisdiction, have suggested that government-appointed "community representatives" attend each conference. Such community representatives hinder the conference process because they lack real emotional involvement with the offender, the victim or the incident. They bring little to the conference that cannot be provided by those who have an emotional stake in the incident, and they often convey righteousness and moral superiority that dampens the free expression of emotion by the other participants.

I fear that government will interfere with the gradual spread of conferencing in North America by trying to legislate and regulate conferencing, rather than letting it be adopted as a grassroots innovation in each jurisdiction. To date, conferencing has been implemented in schools and police departments and court systems when there is enough local support for the concept. It requires no formal legislative action, only guidelines as to what range of situations can be conferenced. Those of us who marvel at the power of this simple and elegant process hope that it will never be compromised and complicated by the heavy hand of government.

In New Zealand, conferencing was invented by legislation, not through experimentation. Some experienced facilitators in that country have expressed their frustration with the rigid legal and bureaucratic requirements imposed on their process by politicians and administrators who have no direct experience with conferencing. These New Zealand facilitators see some significant advantages in the Wagga Wagga conferencing model that Terry O'Connell developed through trial and error, but they may not adopt that approach.

Ironically, similar political and bureaucratic constraints have ended conferencing by police officers in Wagga Wagga and the rest of the state of New South Wales. Politicians and the administration of the large police force that serves the entire state have ruled against police officers doing conferences, despite the compelling evidence provided by two excellent Australian research studies that support the merits of police conferencing.

Only when we have a depth of experience with conferencing and the process is thoroughly understood and supported by both practitioners and the populace should we consider legislation. Issues such as protecting the confidentiality of information brought to light in conferences would benefit from legislative clarification, but we need to allow the innovation to mature before we pass laws about it.

In many instances government need not be involved at all. In Vermont, representatives of the Department of Corrections and other government officials have been discussing "community justice centers," which would provide, among other things, a supervised pool of screened and trained volunteers to run conferences as needed for police, schools, courts and corrections. A retailer who catches a young shoplifter, for example, might opt to take the culprit directly to the community justice center for a conference without involving the police.

Community Empowerment

At this point the community justice center is only in the "brainstorming" phase of development, but if you think the idea is far-fetched, consider the following story. A youth vandalized a neighborhood tree house and stole a television set that he found there. When he was discovered and admitted his offense, the police advised the families in the neighborhood that they would like to handle the case as a restorative conference. By the time the police officer handling the case began to contact families, he discovered that the neighbors and their children got together with the offender and his family and had successfully run their own restorative conference. One of the neighbors had previously attended a restorative conference for a different matter and felt confident that he could run the conference. So instead of waiting for the police, the neighbors "took the law into their own hands." Unlike vigilantes seeking vengeance, the neighborhood used restorative justice, which repairs the harm and allows the offender to be reintegrated in the community.

Kay Pranis, restorative justice planner for the Minnesota Department of Corrections, suggests that restorative justice requires a partnership between government and community in which government is responsible for legality while the community provides morality. The government has the responsibility for oversight and must ensure that the process and outcome stay within the bounds of law. The community can convey a unique sense of right and wrong, based not on fear of punishment, but based on a feeling of mutual regard for others with whom one feels connected. Conferencing done in the right spirit by citizens themselves, as exemplified by the neighbors who handled the tree-house incident on their own, can build healthier communities.

The Royal Canadian Mounted Police have adopted conferencing for juvenile offenses as a community policing initiative. But the RCMP is focusing its efforts on training police officers to teach community volunteers how to facilitate conferences. Then police officers will process cases and refer them to the community to facilitate.

Government cannot do it all. We need to recognize the limits of laws and police and courts and prisons and the critical need for a sense of community. Conferencing can help move us in that direction by turning wrongdoing into an opportunity to build community.

Ice Fishing

One winter night a group of teen-age boys vandalized several recreational ice-fishing houses. The structures, which were set up on the frozen surface of a local lake every year, sheltered the fishermen from the extreme cold. Some of these houses, which were quite substantial, even providing sleeping and cooking facilities.

Although the offenders were identified, the public prosecutor felt he could not proceed with the case because he did not have enough information to charge each offender with specific damage to a specific ice-fishing house. Instead, the local police handled the case with one large restorative conference.

Henry, one of the owners, was particularly upset that the offenders were not going to court. He and his son, Henry Jr., now an adult, had spent many years fishing on the lake. Their ice-fishing house had evolved into an elaborate structure. The house was seriously damaged. Henry wanted the culprits punished. He angrily warned that he would not be satisfied with the conference.

The night of the conference the offenders and their parents met the victims and their families. Although all lived in the same suburb, few in the victims' and offenders' groups knew each other.

The facilitator asked each of the youths to tell what happened. Each youth individually admitted his part in the vandalism and expressed remorse for his actions.

Then the owners and their family members were asked to tell how the vandalism had affected them. The facilitator avoided asking Henry, the angriest owner, to speak first. When it was Henry's turn he chose not to speak. Henry Jr., however, spoke eloquently about how he and his father had built and refined their ice-fishing house over the years and how it represented the happy memories of those times he and his father had spent together. His comments touched the hearts of everyone at the conference and conveyed the realization that the ice-fishing houses were more than shelters to their owners.

The conference proceeded smoothly through the agreement phase. The young offenders appropriately apologized and they or their parents paid for the damages that night, while still at the conference. When the facilitator asked if anyone had anything further to say, Henry indicated that he wanted to speak.

"I know it may seem strange, but I want to thank you boys for what you've done. I was very angry with you and I wasn't happy about this conference. But if none of this had happened, I might never have heard my son talk about how much all those years of fishing and working together meant to him. So I want to thank you for giving me that opportunity."

Then Henry looked around the room at all of the offenders and said, "I'd also like to invite all of you boys and your fathers, as soon as the damage is repaired, to come ice fishing with us."

20

Conclusion

We, as citizens, must help revolutionize our society's response to wrongdoing. We cannot wait for the politicians to find a new strategy. Though they claim to be our leaders, they seem to follow trends rather than set them.

In the decade between 1986 and 1996 the American prison population more than doubled, from 744,208 to 1,630,940. The Bureau of Justice Statistics projects another 51 percent increase in the prison population by the year 2000. No other industrial nation in the world has incarcerated such a large percentage of its population, yet they have lower crime rates.

Our schools are experiencing more disciplinary problems, more violence, truancy and dropouts. While American schools fine parents for their children's truancy and adopt "zero tolerance" policies, which suspend and expel more students, the negative statistics grow.

Victims are revictimized by our current processes. Offenses are defined as violations against the state or the school, so criminal justice and school discipline fail to repair the harm done to individuals and communities. Scant attention is paid to healing. The focus is on punishment.

Relying on punishment in courts and schools, we stigmatize offenders and create outcasts. Punishment does not foster understanding and empathy for victims; it fosters resentment and alienation. How ironic that offenders see themselves as victims.

In the criminal justice system, particularly, we are inconsistent. Courts are so overwhelmed that they often minimize offenses with plea bargaining and probation, without appropriately confronting offenders or making them repair the harm they have done to their victims.

We need a system of justice that holds offenders accountable for their actions and provides meaningful consequences. Offenders must face what they have done and those they have harmed. Certainly there are offenders who are so dangerous that they must be confined, but we are incarcerating far too many, wasting money and ruining lives. We need to look at our dilemma with cool clear eyes. Let us abandon slogans like "if you do the crime, you do the time" and reassess our failed policies. If things are not getting better, common sense dictates that we do something different. Real justice is different.

We can raise our voices as citizens and voters. Through letters to the editor, talk radio, other public forums and at the ballot box, we can tell judges and legislators and governors and school boards to support the development of conferencing. And we can sing the praises of those who already have done so. As employers and supervisors and employees, we can encourage conferencing in the workplace. As police, attorneys, judges, probation, parole and corrections officers we can open ourselves and the criminal justice system to conferencing. As educators and academicians and administrators, we can foster conferencing in our classrooms and schools. As parents, we can support conferencing in schools, day-care centers, camps, church groups, scout troops and other youth organizations. We can volunteer to be trained and facilitate conferences.

In the many years since I went to juvenile court for the Uncle Marty's Sneaker Barn burglary, I have never been so hopeful about meaningful reform as I am now. The road to real justice will be long and difficult, but I am encouraged by the people who have responded enthusiastically and decided to make the journey with us.

Of course, there are still skeptics. Even when we cite the favorable research results achieved to date, naysayers raise new fears and objections. We suggest that they observe a conference. When they do, as many skeptics have, their objections will melt away. They become advocates.

For me, my intuition was the critical factor in deciding to create the Real Justice program. While I acknowledge the value of research, I know that conferencing will gain momentum and become an established practice, not as a result of scientific evaluation, but because it feels right. In the closing hours of a three-day restorative justice seminar in Washington, D.C., some of the participants expressed the need for more research to evaluate processes like conferencing. In the midst of the discussion an elder Native American gentleman rose to speak. He looked around the group, shaking his head and smiling, then spoke slowly.

"You don't have to do research to prove that it works. You just have to do it. And then, if the sun seems to shine a little brighter, you'll know that it works."

Epilogue

Much has happened since 1997 when I wrote the *Real Justice* book. Real Justice and its licensees around the world have trained thousands of people to facilitate restorative conferences. Schools, community agencies, youth programs, police, courts, prisons and businesses have used the formal restorative conference to respond to crime and wrongdoing.

We have been challenged by the sobering fact that meaningful change is difficult to achieve and even harder to sustain. Nonetheless, restorative conferences and related restorative practices, such as sentencing circles and family group conferences for child protection and family violence, are gradually spreading. Importantly, we began to realize that restorative justice could readily be incorporated informally into people's daily lives, beyond the use of formal processes. In the surveys conducted by the Real Justice program following our early trainings, we learned that while most of our trainees had not facilitated a formal conference, many were using the language and underlying principles of restorative conferencing. Educators who had been trained, instead of handing out punishments, began to address incidents of school wrongdoing by getting students to think about what they had done, whom they had affected and how they might repair the harm they had caused. Real Justice trainees, in parenting their own children, were conducting informal restorative conferences.

We developed the "Social Discipline Window" (see below) to describe our new understanding of restorative strategies. Those who use only high control in response to wrongdoing, but provide little support, are "punitive." Their leadership style is "authoritarian" because they primarily do things TO people. Those who only respond to wrongdoing with high support and little control are "permissive." Their leadership style is "paternalistic" because they primarily do things FOR people. The neglectful leader who does NOT do anything in response to wrongdoing is simply "irresponsible."

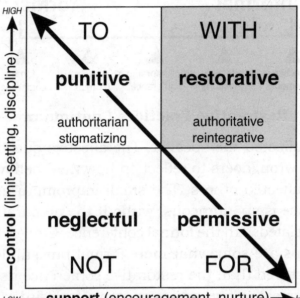

Social Discipline Window

Those who respond to wrongdoing with both high control and high support are "restorative." Their leadership style is "authoritative" because they do things WITH people. Although they have authority, they engage and empower people, allowing them to be heard and to have a say in the outcome.

We developed the "Restorative Practices Continuum" (see below) to describe the range of possible restorative approaches. Beginning with the most informal practices on the left side of the continuum, the affective statement simply expresses emotion, telling wrongdoers how their behavior

Restorative Practices Continuum

has affected the speaker. The affective question asks wrongdoers to reflect on how their behavior has affected others. The small impromptu conference is spontaneous, without the preparation associated with the formal conference. Circles and groups are somewhat more formal but still less structured than the restorative conference itself.

As restorative practices move from informal to formal, they tend to involve more people, take more time to carry out, require more preparation and are more structured. They also tend to have more impact.

We began to use the term "restorative practices" because we realized that restorative justice is only one of many areas of human activity that can benefit from a restorative approach. It is also relevant to education, social work, psychology, counseling, parenting, organizational leadership—anything that involves the management and motivation of human beings and the need to establish social discipline.

The fundamental thesis underlying restorative practices is that people are happier, more productive, more cooperative and more likely to make positive changes when those in authority do things *with* them, rather than *to* them or *for* them.

We also began to think in terms of proactive and reactive restorative practices. Not only can restorative practices be used to react to wrongdoing, but also their deliberate use before there is any wrongdoing fosters emotional bonds and builds relationships. Using circles, for example, in classroom or business settings, encourages people to express their feelings and personal stories, allowing them to get to know each other and creating a sense of community.

In 1999 I founded the International Institute for Restorative Practices (IIRP), a nonprofit educational organization, to take over the ongoing Real Justice® program and several new programs that were created to spread restorative practices. SaferSanerSchools™ brings restorative practices to education, Family Power[SM] addresses social work and counseling, and Good Company[SM] focuses on organizational management. The IIRP collaborates with the Community Service Foundation and Buxmont Academy, two nonprofit organizations that provide educational, counseling and residential services for delinquent and at-risk youth in eastern Pennsylvania (csfbuxmont.org) and which serve as demonstration programs for the use of restorative practices.

The international conferences about restorative practices that began under the auspices of the Real Justice program in 1998 in North America are now run by the IIRP and are held on several continents at more frequent intervals. The IIRP has produced a variety of new educational resources about restorative practices, including several websites (iirp.org, realjustice.org, safersanerschools.org, familypower.org and goodcompanyonline.org) and an email publication called the *Restorative Practices eForum*, which has thousands of subscribers throughout the world.

We have established program branches of the IIRP in several countries: IIRP UK, IIRP Canada, Real Justice Australia and the Community Service Foundation of Hungary. We also have Real Justice licensees in China, Costa Rica, the Netherlands, New Zealand, Sweden, Thailand and in many locations in the United States and Canada.

In 2006 the Pennsylvania Department of Education authorized the IIRP as a specialized research and graduate degree–granting institution, the first graduate school in the world wholly dedicated to restorative practices.

The IIRP is dedicated to building a global alliance that fosters the use of restorative practices across professional and national boundaries. We invite you to join us.

—Ted Wachtel, 2007

References

Braithwaite, J. (1989). *Crime, shame and reintegration*. Cambridge, UK: Cambridge University Press.

Moore, D.B. (1997). Pride, shame and empathy in peer relations: New theory and practice in education and juvenile justice. In K. Rigby & P. Slee (Eds.), *Children's peer relations*. London: Routledge.

Moore, D.B. & Forsythe, L. (1995). *A new approach to juvenile justice: An evaluation of restorative conferencing in Wagga Wagga*. A report to the Criminology Research Council, Wagga Wagga, New South Wales, Australia: Centre for Rural Social Research, Charles Sturt University-Riverina.

Nathanson, D.L. (1992). *Shame and pride: Affect, sex and the birth of the self*. New York: Norton & Company.

National Organization for Victim Assistance Newsletter (1997), Vol. 17, No. 11.

Zehr, H. (1990). *Changing lenses: A new focus for crime and justice*. Scottdale, PA: Herald Press.

Educational Resources

To learn more about books, videos and other resources provided by the IIRP, please go to: www.iirp.org/store.

Conferencing Handbook:
The New Real Justice Training Manual
Book by Terry O'Connell, Ben Wachtel and Ted Wachtel

This official training manual is a clearly conceived procedural guide to coordinating and facilitating conferences, covering the process of selecting cases, inviting participants, making preparations and running the conference itself. It is useful to anyone who wants to learn to facilitate conferences in school, criminal justice and other settings.

Burning Bridges
DVD produced by IIRP/Real Justice

Burning Bridges is a 35-minute documentary about the arson of Mood's Bridge, a historic covered bridge in Bucks County, Pennsylvania, and the restorative conference held in its wake. The IIRP facilitated this emotional meeting, which brought together the six young men who burned down the bridge with their families and members of the community. Using news footage, interviews and video of the actual conference, the documentary tells the story of a community moving through grief and anger to healing.

Facing the Demons
DVD produced by Dee Cameron Co.

Facing the Demons is an hour-long documentary video about the journey of the family and friends of murder victim Michael Marslew and how they confronted two of the men responsible for Michael's death in a restorative conference. It won an award for "best television documentary of 1999" at the 2000 Logies Awards, the Australian equivalent of the Emmy Awards.

Conferencing for Serious Offenses: An Exploration
DVD set produced by IIRP/Real Justice

This thought-provoking, interactive, "do-it-yourself" seminar package provides DVD videos (and a CD-ROM with printable Facilitator Guide and Participant Handout) for a group of professionals, students or others to examine the use of restorative conferencing in response to serious offenses. This seminar is not intended to train participants to facilitate restorative conferences, but to enhance their understanding of the potential and the implications of conferencing for serious offenses.

Four School Conferences: A Composite View
DVD set produced by IIRP/Real Justice

By combining footage of actual Real Justice conferences for offenses ranging from truancy and leaving school grounds to drug possession and bringing a knife onto a school bus, this video provides a realistic view of conferencing. All four conferences were videotaped at alternative schools operated by the Community Service Foundation and Buxmont Academy in eastern Pennsylvania.

Toxic Talk: From Betrayal to Trust in a Workplace
DVD produced by IIRP/Good Company .

Toxic Talk shows an actual restorative conference following a workplace incident, where staff members demeaned their supervisor behind her back. The conference, by providing all involved with a structured setting to express their emotions freely, transformed negative feelings into positive ones, restored relationships and created a healthier work environment. This stands in stark contrast to the way most workplace conflicts are handled, where negative feelings fester and toxic talk persists.

Join the IIRP's Restorative Practices eForum

To receive articles about restorative practices efforts in criminal justice, family and social services and the workplace, join the IIRP's Restorative Practices eForum.

You'll receive occasional short emails including brief summaries of significant articles, research reports and information about upcoming restorative practices events — with links to full articles. Become part of a worldwide network of people who believe in the possibility of meaningful change.

eForum emails do not include attachments. We do not share our eForum database, so you will receive no spam.

Sign up at www.iirp.org/eforum.

About the IIRP

This book is a publication of the International Institute for Restorative Practices (IIRP), which provides education, international conferences, print, video and other resources in the emerging field of restorative practices.

The IIRP Graduate School provides master's degree and certificate programs for educators and others who work with children and youth. To learn more about the IIRP Graduate School, please go to: www.iirp.org.

The IIRP Training and Consulting Division is a leading provider of restorative practices training, consulting and resource materials throughout the world. The IIRP and its related organizations have trained thousands of individuals in education, criminal justice, and social and human services since its inception in 1995. To learn more about the IIRP Training and Consulting Division, please go to: www.iirp.org/training.